The Long Surrender

Minneapolis

FIRST EDITION MAY 2022
The Long Surrender: A Memoir About Losing My Religion
Copyright © 2022 by Brian Rush McDonald
All rights reserved

For information, write to Calumet Editions,
6800 France Avenue South, Suite 370, Edina, MN 55435

Printed in the United States of America.
10 9 8 7 6 5 4 3 2 1
ISBN: 978-1-950743-80-3

Cover and interior design: Gary Lindberg

Front cover etching: The Neophyte (First Experience of the Monastery)
by Gustave Doré, ca. 1866–68. Courtesy of Yale University Art Gallery.

The Long Surrender

A Memoir About Losing My Religion

Brian Rush McDonald

Wisdom
Editions
Minneapolis

Table of Contents

Note to the Reader

The names of individuals mentioned throughout the book are their actual names. In a few instances, a pseudonym is used to protect the privacy of a particular individual. In most cases, only the first name is used. In one instance, a first name was changed to avoid confusion with another person with the same first name. When well-known individuals are mentioned, the entire name is given. The writer has attempted to remain faithful to the facts and events as memory permits.

All Biblical quotations are from the King James Version of the Bible unless otherwise indicated.

In spelling Chinese names and words, there has been no attempt to follow any particular system of Romanization. The author uses the spelling that was commonly used for a name or word at the time or has spelled it in such a manner as to be readable for readers of English.

1

I look at the single sheet of paper in my hands, one piece of typing paper folded in half. All of the notes I made during the week have been condensed here. As a minister for nearly twenty-five years, longer if I count seminary, I rarely delivered a sermon that was written out word for word. That's not my style. But I have always gone over my notes sufficiently so that I deliver them as planned, glancing at the outline only occasionally.

Early Sunday morning, I have a cup of tea on the table beside me. Kathy is still asleep. It's the two of us now. Our three children are out of the nest; two in college, the other in the army. I've always enjoyed rising early to pray and read scripture. I love the quiet of dawn when there are no distractions, and my mind is clear. I have written Chinese characters under each of the main points enabling me to state them clearly. The rest I will translate into Mandarin as I speak, formulating phrases in my mind.

"Jazzie wants to go out," Kathy calls from the top of the stairs. Our toy poodle comes trotting down the stairs. Holding my tea mug in one hand, the leash in the other, I make my way down our street. Dew clings to the grass; the Bradford pear blossoms adorn trees along our lane, and birds conduct a concert. I greet a neighbor walking her dog.

"Beautiful day, isn't it?" she says.

"It really is," I say.

When I go inside and unclip her leash, Jazzie scampers back upstairs, no doubt to reclaim her place in bed. I pour Kathy a cup of coffee and take it to her. I refill my mug with tea and return to my recliner. My open Bible in my lap shows parallel English and Chinese on each page. Today, I weigh each word that I will say even more carefully than usual.

I arrive at the church before anyone else. Kathy will come a little later. The natural siding on the building makes the church blend in with the wooded lot. The wild heather growing on the portion of the land between the church and a busy road gives it a rustic feel in an otherwise suburban area.

Next to the lane leading into the church is a sign: Westwood Baptist Church. Another sign near it, written in English and Chinese, says Northern Virginia Chinese Baptist Mission.

I park in one of the spaces marked "Church Staff" and go to my study and close the door. I have always seen my study as a refuge, a sanctuary within the sanctuary, in every church I have served. Over the years, I have collected many theological and biblical reference books. There are sets of commentaries on the various sections of the Bible and titles on various theological subjects.

My eyes fall on a box sitting on the floor. It is marked "Greek and Hebrew Reference" in large letters. My thoughts go to the day in seminary when I received my copy of the Hebrew scriptures, one of the heftiest books in my study, an impressive tome. I recall the hours I spent trying to read the ancient text.

My books have always comforted me as I sat in my study each day doing the work of the church. They hold the wisdom of those who have gone before me, those who have probed the depths of this faith. I like to think they represent the knowledge that I have acquired over the years, knowledge that I have drawn upon in order to relate my faith to those under my pastoral care.

The time for the morning worship service draws closer. Members who have duties arrive. I hear the choir rehearse as I walk toward the worship area.

"Good morning, Pastor," someone says warmly, and I respond in kind.

"Mu shi zao!" another says, bowing slightly.

I take my place at the front of the church and look out over the congregation. The people sitting before me are mostly from China. A few are from other Chinese-speaking places such as Taiwan, Singapore or Hong Kong. For many of these people, this is the only church they have ever attended. I am the only pastor they have ever known. I baptized many of them. For so many years, I have treasured being called pastor and devoted myself to being the shepherd this title indicates.

Church is a community for these people, a place where they can be around others who speak their language and share their cultural backgrounds. The children and teenagers of the congregation who prefer to speak English attend the service of our host church in another part of the building. Often after the morning service, there is a potluck lunch, and everyone stays and eats. No one is eager to leave.

Many of these congregants originally came to the US for college or graduate school. There are engineers, computer scientists, linguists, statisticians and others in a variety of specialized fields. Quite a few have doctoral degrees. Others work in restaurants or run small businesses. There are also the elderly parents who have come from China to live with their children and grandchildren. In this place, they receive strength and hope.

I stand at the pulpit, open my bible and place the folded sheet of paper beside it. The biblical text is that of the prodigal son.

"While we know this as a story about a wayward son, it is actually a story about a welcoming and compassionate father." I explain that people often see God as angry and eager to punish sinners. But the story of the prodigal son shows us a father who waits for his child to return and is willing to forgive and restore his child into his home.

"God is a merciful, forgiving father. God considers every person to be his child and desires that each person know him," I tell them. The congregants look up at me, eagerly accepting this reassuring message.

I have studied the complexities of Christian theology extensively. I have read books that conceptualize the Christian faith using various theological frameworks. I have searched for a theological system that I can enthusiastically embrace, even if it is not what I was taught.

I have always taken matters of faith seriously. *Have I taken it too seriously? Why do I agonize over certain facets of Christian teaching while other ministers appear rather cavalier as they discuss the intricacies of Christian theology?*

My message concludes with a prayer. The service proceeds as normal. A member leads the congregation in a hymn, followed by the week's announcements. The offering is received.

I step down from the platform and stand in front of the pulpit, level with the congregation. As the final hymn concludes, people look at me expectantly. They know this as the time when I ask for heads to be bowed, and I raise my hand to deliver the blessing. I have various benedictions written in the back flyleaf of my Bible, though I mostly know them by heart.

"The Lord bless you and keep you; the Lord make his face shine upon you and be gracious to you; the Lord turn his face toward you and give you peace. Amen."

The familiar rhythm of the service comforts congregants as they leave church for another week. Today, this rhythm is broken.

"I have something to say before concluding this morning's service." My voice shakes slightly. *I don't have to resign. Do I really want to walk away from the congregation?*

"I am resigning as your pastor; today is my last day." Most appear puzzled and confused. Some turn to look at each other with searching expressions. I offer no explanation.

"Mo dao, san hui" (please meditate in silence before leaving), I say. Congregants bow their heads silently. An uneasy feeling settles on the rows of people. On a typical Sunday, I would walk quietly to the back of the church, where I then greet each congregant as they exit the worship area. I can call each of the one hundred or so attendees by both their Chinese and English names.

On this day in 2004, I do not greet each person. I don't want to answer their questions. I later realized this may have been unkind of me, but I couldn't face it. While heads are bowed in silence, I nod at Kathy to join me, and we go to my study in another wing of the church. We had packed up most things last night. We load the few remaining boxes into my car.

"We'll put your office stuff in the garage for now, but I want to convert one of the spare bedrooms into a study for you," Kathy says.

Now I have no job or career. I have never done anything other than being a missionary and pastor. I have spent the past thirty years of my life pursuing this calling, and I am willingly walking away from it. I wonder to myself how a country boy from Alabama who dreamed of being a musician ended up being a fundamentalist preacher. And why did the faith that seemed so positive when I was young become so toxic to me?

We make the twenty-minute drive to our home. As we pull into the driveway, Jazzie looks out the front window; her body vibrates with the exuberant wagging of her tail. We're home.

Part I
Good Boy

2

My parents looked at architectural drawings spread out on the kitchen table. Daddy worked at the shipyard in Pascagoula, Mississippi, about forty miles from our home in Mobile, Alabama, and made these kinds of drawings for his job. The lines he had drawn on the paper with a ruler and compass showed notations made in tiny, meticulously written letters.

I had seen Daddy make this type of drawing before when he built something or made some modification to our home, which he constructed mostly himself in the 1940s. At the time, he used lumber and materials from houses that had been torn down, pulling out nails and knocking old mortar off bricks to reuse.

Our home was in a fairly rural area on seven acres of land. Only one acre of it was cleared for our yard. Mobile is known for its azaleas, and we had some of the most beautiful bushes in the neighborhood. Thick woods that characterized the terrain near the Gulf coast covered the remainder of the land.

In 1963 the woods behind our house were a place of adventure. Once, we built a fort out of old lumber and fallen limbs. We caught tadpoles in the creek, which became a torrent during the heavy summer rains and washed up all kinds of things: toys, tools, old shoes.

There was a barn for our horse on the edge of the woods behind our house. Gypsy was a pinto, a multi-colored horse like the one Little Joe rode on *Bonanza*. Some neighbors had horses as well.

We strung two strands of barbed wire around the perimeter of six acres, and Gypsy roamed the woods. Occasionally a fallen limb knocked down a portion of the fence, and Gypsy wandered out. We later retrieved her after receiving a phone call saying that she was grazing in a neighbor's yard.

I fed Gypsy twice a day, and each Saturday mucked out the paddock. Sometimes the girl who lived across the street came over, and we braided Gypsy's mane and gave her carrots and sugar cubes.

***

The drawings Mom and Daddy looked at were for a little house they planned to build on our property for my maternal grandmother. It was going to be a two-room/one-bathroom cottage about one hundred feet from the main house. We called her Granny, saying she looked like Granny Clampett of the *Beverly Hillbillies*.

Before moving to the cottage on our property, she lived in an upstairs apartment closer to town. When visiting her there, I played with her treadle sewing machine—she disengaged the belt that drove the mechanism and let me pump away. Occasionally my toe found its way between the iron treadle and the floor, and I yelled out in pain. I liked to go through the box I found in one of the sewing machine drawers that contained buttons of all shapes and sizes. There was a device that looked like a ball on a stick which she used to darn socks in the old days.

Each Friday, after picking up my brother Joe and me from school, my mother picked up Granny and took her to buy groceries at the A&P, an event Granny referred to as going to the Tea Store— Atlantic and Pacific Tea Company.

Daddy hired a carpenter to do the bulk of the work. Joe, age fourteen, became his helper. The delivery of the building materials excited me as much as if it had been toys—lumber, bricks, wiring, paint. The carpenter had a big fan to produce a breeze in the stifling

Alabama summer heat. It didn't have a grill for safety, and Joe severely cut several of his fingers when he accidentally put his hand into the whirling blades. That ended his job as a carpenter's assistant.

I couldn't imagine anything more exciting than Granny moving into a cottage in our yard. Granny had never lived in a rural area and was unaccustomed to the very dark nights and the sounds that went along with living surrounded by woods, so I often spent the night with her in the cottage. This allowed me to see and experience the habits of a person who had been born in a previous century.

Not more than five feet tall, Granny was rugged in her own way. When roaches appeared—a constant battle in Alabama—she squashed them with her thumb. She told of wringing the necks of chickens and straining milk from a family cow. She wore loose-fitting stockings held up with elastic garters right below the knee.

Everything edible in Granny's house was kept in the refrigerator to protect it from bugs. Cookies were always cold, and so was bread. A piece of toast had four slabs of hard margarine on the surface—the bread burned in the oven broiler before the margarine melted.

Born in 1880, Granny had been orphaned as a young child and was raised in the homes of much older siblings. She was proud to have finished second-class high school, as she called it. When her sister Cora failed a grade, Granny whipped her sister with a switch all the way home.

Granny's toes were all bunched up and overlapped each other, something she said was due to wearing shoes too small as a child. She laughed as she showed me her toenails, each looking like a little hard anthill. One of nine children, her older brothers all succumbed to tuberculosis in middle age. She and two sisters lived into their nineties.

At night before bed, Granny took down the white bun atop her head and braided it into a long queue down her back. Her teeth, which she used only for weddings, funerals, or other auspicious occasions, were kept in a container in the bathroom. She had dropped and broken them at some point, so when not being worn, they were held together with chewing gum. When she showed them to me, we laughed hysterically. Once, her sister borrowed her teeth to wear to a wedding.

Before going to bed, I said my prayers aloud. "Now I lay me down to sleep, I pray the Lord my soul to keep. If I should die before I wake, I pray the Lord my soul to take. God bless Mama, Daddy, Joe and Granny." What God bless meant, I never really considered. Granny beamed with approval when I said my prayers.

On Sunday mornings, I often went to the cottage, and Granny and I turned on the local TV channel and listened to The Alabama Boys or The Gulf Coast Quartet, gospel quartets that came on each week. Most of the songs were about heaven, the pearly gates or the streets of gold. Each group of male performers included one who could sing really high and one who could sing really low. I waited with anticipation for the end of a song when the bass singer, who was usually tall and skinny, might slide his voice down to a really low note.

I liked Sunday school, the stories interested me, and there were bright colored cut-out figures. Everyone dressed up. I received a new set of Sunday clothes each Easter. The teachers praised us for being there and called when I didn't show up for a while.

"Even though I am Methodist, being a Baptist is a good thing because John was a Baptist," Granny often said. She wanted to hear about Sunday school when I got home, concluding that I was such a *good boy*.

Granny rarely attended church herself—she said it was because she was hard of hearing. We didn't like to take her to church, anyway. She might think she was whispering and say something like, "I believe that preacher is the ugliest man I've ever seen."

Granny's hearing deficit manifested itself in humorous ways. Rather than saying that she didn't understand something, she instead repeated what it sounded like to her.

"We are going to the store," I might say.

"You dropped it on the floor?" she replied.

"He went to bed," I would say.

"He dropped dead?" she exclaimed.

***

"Come get your breakfast," Granny called as she stood at the front door of the cottage. She wasn't calling for me; she was calling for the animals. Cats came running from every direction. Buckshot, our Old Yeller-looking dog, came trotting on three legs. The fourth leg had been injured during one of his car-chasing adventures, and he held it up, sometimes continuing to chase cars on three legs.

After gulping down his food, Buckshot returned to his favorite sunbathing spot, the front walk of our house. Lying on his back with all four feet in the air, his ample maleness prominently displayed, more than one visitor asked if he were alive. He had a kind of southern charm, I thought. Daddy hated him.

"They love me because I feed them," Granny said.

I knocked on Granny's front door as hard as I could, making sure she heard. I then looked in the door's window and saw her mumble to herself as she got out of her rocker and shuffled her way to the door. I hid in the bushes.

After opening the door, she began to look for the source of the knock. When she stepped out onto the porch, I jumped up out of the bushes and startled her. She jumped at my sudden appearance, and the scare caused her to pass gas audibly. We both then broke into laughter, and she began to hold herself. "Oh, oh, I'm going to wet myself." I loved teasing her like this.

"Bri-ooooooooon! Get in this house right now before you get struck by lightning." Granny feared thunder and lightning. I pretended not to hear her for a while. Then I began to amble back to the house. When lightning flashed again, I fell to the ground as if I had been struck.

"Gawd is going to punish you for treating your poor old grandmother like that," she admonished me, wagging her finger. She didn't stay mad long, and we were laughing again in a few minutes.

One Christmas, my cousin got a Creepy Crawlers set. We cooked up rubber bugs and put them on the floor in Granny's little house.

"Look, Granny, a roach," we pointed.

"Kill it," she said. "Step on it quick." She then went to get the broom to sweep it out the door. After a while, she caught on, but we did it again and again.

There was a well-worn path from our back door to the front door of the cottage. I took Granny a plate of supper each night. On more than one occasion, in my haste to get there, the food slid onto the ground, and I had to return to get more. Usually, everything on the plate was red from the pickled beets we had for every meal, no matter what the main dish was. Occasionally, Mom forgot to send her supper. Around 8:30 the phone rang.

"I guess I'm not getting any supper, so I'm going to bed." she said, stoically.

***

"Aunt Cora is coming to stay for a while," Granny said. Now things really got interesting. Granny and Aunt (we pronounced it ain't) Cora were both in their eighties, and neither had any teeth. Aunt Cora brought a bag full of baby food in jars because she couldn't swallow solid food.

It was hard to believe they grew up in the same home. Granny never used anything close to a bad word. Aunt Cora, on the other hand, could use some rather saucy language. I found it to be quite educational.

"Don't say that in front of Brian, Cora," Granny said. "He'll tell his daddy." Granny feared offending Daddy, reasoning he might not allow her to continue to live there.

"I don't give a snap," Aunt Cora retorted. She was a bigger woman than Granny. Having had nine children, her once ample, braless breasts now hung low. One day, trying to make me laugh, Aunt Cora grabbed two handfuls of her loose-fitting dress and held them up, squeezing them as if milking a cow's teats.

"DON'T DO THAT, CORA!" Granny erupted, trembling with anger.

Any interest I showed in church or religion was praised by Granny. She often said that her husband, my grandfather, who died before I was born, was such a good man and was looked up to in the church. I liked hearing that I might be like him.

3

I followed Daddy like a shadow as he built and repaired things. I went with him to the hardware store or lumber yard on Saturdays. Sometimes I rode in the trailer that he pulled behind the car as we drove out into the country to dump unwanted items. I loved searching through stuff that other people had discarded.

Daddy had patience with me. He allowed me to help as he built things. I even used the power saw. When I bent nails trying to hammer them, he didn't get angry. He showed me how to straighten them. He let me sit in his lap and steer the car on the country road where we lived. Once I wanted to carry a watermelon, I dropped it, splitting it into pieces.

"That's alright, we were going to cut it anyway," he said.

I often rode my bike to the end of our street and waited for Daddy's ride to drop him off when he got home from his job thirty miles away. He always carried a thermos of water and an umbrella. I rode circles around him as we walked the half-mile to our house.

"Daddy, why weren't you in the military like my friends' fathers?" I asked Daddy one day.

"Well, I was sick during that time," he said.

I asked Mom about this, and she said Daddy had a nervous breakdown and was unable to serve in the military. What this meant, I didn't know.

Daddy was a capable person, but he tended to take a back seat when in a group of people, saying little. Apparently, before his nervous breakdown, he had been an extremely gregarious person. Mom said she was engaged to another man when Daddy talked her into marrying him. We had a photograph of Daddy doing a fancy dive from a high diving board, something I couldn't imagine him doing.

When Daddy needed to know how to repair or build something, he went to the library and studied the matter until he understood it. Sometimes he sat and read the encyclopedia, not searching for anything in particular. But, he was detached emotionally. He didn't really try to understand what was going on in my or Joe's life. If Mom told me to show Daddy my report card, all he said was, "that's good."

I later learned Daddy didn't work for several years early in his married life. According to Mom, he often lay in bed crying. If he got up, he walked around the yard, his shoes not tied. A doctor told her that he was criminally insane.

"Why would anyone say that about Daddy?" I asked, incredulous. Mom said it was because Daddy told the doctor that he had a recurring image in his mind of hitting his wife with an ax. When I related this to an elderly relative many years later, he quipped, "Haven't we all?"

The doctor recommended that Mom take him to New Orleans to have electroconvulsive therapy. I don't know how long the treatment lasted. Mom said there was no apparent change in Daddy immediately afterward.

"One day, he got up and said he was going to look for a job," Mom said. A few months later, he returned to normal. He got back on his feet and ultimately led a productive life. Daddy never mentioned the shock treatment. Whether he didn't remember it or didn't want to talk about it, we never knew. He lived to be eighty-seven years old.

Sometimes Joe let me play with him and his friends, but the five-year age difference made it hard. Joe was athletic and often won competitions during school field day. There were photos of him holding ribbons, and as far I knew, it could have been the Olympics. I tried to boost my chances of being chosen for sports teams by noting that I was Joe McDonald's brother. It got some notice, but my performance didn't measure up.

Once when riding on the back of Joe's bicycle, my bare foot found its way into the spokes. I screamed. Feeling badly about the mishap, Joe made a crutch by sawing off a limb from a tree and wrapping rags around the part that went under my arm.

"Joe, it's for you. Cindy again," Mom said as she covered the receiver with her hand. The telephone hung on the wall in the kitchen, across from the kitchen table. Cindy pursued Joe relentlessly.

"Tell her I'm not here," Joe mouthed the words. Most times, he talked to Cindy or other girls by stretching the kitchen wall phone into the adjoining dining room and closing the door.

"You are going to ruin the phone cord doing that," Daddy yelled. "Get off the phone, someone may be trying to call us."

Joe and I shared a room. We split it down the middle to keep things separate. Joe had pictures of motorcycles on the wall. He laid in bed at night making the sound of a motorcycle going through its gears. Once, Joe laid on his back with his pants and underwear off and held a match to his butthole to see if it would shoot out a flame when he farted. All it did was blow out the match. When it was time to go to sleep, Joe told me to get up and turn off the light.

"If you don't get up and turn off that light by the time I count to ten, I am going to come over there and cave in your head." He made other threats. "I'm going to lay an oyster on your head." This meant coughing up a wad and spitting it across the room at me. He really did this once and I heard it hit the wall. After that I always turned off the light.

Later we got a phone extension in our room. With this, Mom and Daddy didn't know we were on the phone unless they happened to pick up the kitchen phone. When I was in junior high, I talked on the phone with girls for long periods of time, often saying little or nothing, listening to each other breathe.

Mom operated a kindergarten, and all of us participated in the maintenance and upkeep of the old building: painting, cleaning, mowing the lawn. Mom loved to have fun. She tried to do whatever Joe and I did. She fell off Gypsy and broke her ankle. Once, she tried to ride my minibike, fell and cut her fingers badly. She attempted every kind of craft that one could imagine. Ceramics, finger painting, making a turkey picture out of all kinds of seeds, needlepoint, counted cross-stitch, folding the Readers Digest to make choir figures or the phone book to make a Christmas tree.

Mom played the piano, claiming she only had one lesson as a child. She played mostly by ear. As a youth, she heard someone play "In the Sweet Bye and Bye" with all kinds of variations. She practiced that song throughout her life, even into her seventies. She could play and sing at the same time when she led her students. "This land is your land, this land is my land . . ." She belted out the lyrics as her hands boom-chucked across the keys, sometimes landing in the wrong place.

Mom knew how to call square dancing. "Smoke on the water, on the land, and the sea, allemande left your partner, turn around and go back three, and then a left, right, left hand turn all the way around . . ." As a young adult, she learned how to dance and call square dance. She started a square dance club in Mobile called the Alabama Allemanders, which was said to be the first such club in the state.

Daddy either couldn't dance or wouldn't try, so she became a caller. I only remember seeing her actually call a dance on one occasion. Standing on a stool with a microphone in her hand, she sang out the instructions. "Swing your partner to and fro, allemande left and do-si-do."

We lived on a street named Wildwood Place. Woods, fields, the creek, all kinds of bugs and wild animals. Once we dug a hole six feet deep for no particular reason. When a neighbor's horse died, all the kids pitched in to dig a grave next to it for the burial—quite a dig.

"They pushed me in." I lied to Mom, who was upset that I had gotten my shoes and socks wet catching tadpoles in the creek. Any activity that involved getting dirty such as tackle football or wrestling, caused me anxiety when thinking of how to explain to Mom why I had grass stains on my pants, or worse, tore them. My playmates didn't seem to give thought to such matters. My friend Scott sometimes came outside with only his socks on, something I couldn't imagine.

***

"Bring the horse out and let her graze in the yard over the septic tank where that grass is so thick," Daddy said to me one day. Normally I used a rope tied to a concrete block to keep her from wandering too far—she had no desire to run away.

On this day, I found a length of rubber-covered line, used for a clothesline, which I thought was good enough. Ten years old and too lazy to go get a concrete block, I secured the cord to the railing on the back steps of the house. The railing was made of an iron pipe that Daddy cemented at the bottom of the steps and screwed to the wood frame of the house at the top of the steps.

Bored, I decided to sit on Gypsy's back as she grazed contentedly. When I got on her back, she lifted her head and began to trot toward the barn. Without a bridle I had no control. Before I could jump off and stop her, she reached the end of the line tied to the house. The clothesline snapped as if it were a kite string, and I jumped to the ground, thinking the incident was a mere mistake with no consequence.

"What happened?" Daddy shouted as the backdoor flew open, and my ordinarily sedate father came running out. The snapping line must have reverberated throughout the house.

"What did you do?" Daddy yelled.

"Nothing," I said.

"Don't tell me *nothing*," he said, running toward me with a worried look on his face. I tried to explain it to him. "Why on earth would you tie the horse to the house and with a clothesline?" Daddy always had patience with me, and his alarm quickly abated when he realized nothing bad had happened. "Tie the horse properly with a regular length of rope," he said and returned to the house, shaking his head.

I was about eleven years old when Mom started wearing a wig. This started when the parent of one of her kindergarten students gave her a long blonde wig made from real hair in lieu of tuition payment. It sat on a Styrofoam head in her bedroom for a long time.

"Mrs. McDonald, it may not be any of my business, but I just saw a girl riding down the road on Joe's motorcycle," a neighbor on the other end of the telephone line said. Joe and I loved to put on Mom's wig and ride around the neighborhood. Once she discovered wigs, she never had her own hair styled again. She'd drop off the wig at the beauty parlor and pick it up later.

"No wonder you are hot," Daddy said when Mom complained. "You need to take off that wig." Mom's wig-wearing resulted in many hilarious stories. Joe and I tried to knock it off her head. She was good-natured about it.

Going somewhere with friends, like riding our bikes to the drugstore, required pleading with Mom for permission. She made me explain the exact path I would travel, perhaps altering the proposed route if needed, in order to gain her consent. For the most part, I complied. Joe, on the other hand, took a different approach. He did whatever he wanted and dealt with the repercussions later.

***

Sometimes on Sunday, I stayed for preaching after Sunday school. A young boy sitting in church by myself must have struck people as odd. Once I woke to find myself partially stretched out on the pew. Adults stood around me singing. Realizing I had fallen asleep in church, I quickly stood, hoping no one had noticed. Sometimes the preacher told interesting stories. Mostly the minutes crept by as I waited for it to be over. It gave me a good feeling that I had attended.

Marlene and Buddy were childhood friends, almost like relatives. Dimples, their mother, was Mom's childhood friend. Marlene, Buddy and I spent a lot of time together, sometimes going to church. Marlene was one year older than me, and Buddy was one year younger.

When Buddy and I were in church together, we usually sat in the balcony and found things to laugh about. Once when the pastor introduced new members as Mr. and Mrs. Snodgrass, we rolled under the pews stifling giggles. Sometimes we took the rubber rings out of the holes in the back of the pew in front of us where you placed communion cups after drinking the juice. We bounced them on the floor or put them on our fingers as rings.

"If you want to make a decision for Jesus Christ, I invite you to step into the aisle and come to the front of the church when the invitation hymn is sung." The preacher said this after every sermon. "I Surrender All," or "Jesus is Tenderly Calling." These were the kind of hymns we sang during the invitation.

I was excited when there was baptism. I watched through the plexiglass the person's face going under the water. Then the white robe clung to their bodies as they climbed the steps out of the tank. When it was over, the preacher appeared almost immediately back in the sanctuary, miraculously dry.

"All who approve of these dear-ones coming to make a decision today, please say Amen." In the case of membership, the pastor asked for a show of hands to receive them into the church. "Any opposed?" No one ever objected.

After the service, I walked outside where I found Daddy parked. He made no comment about my attendance, positive or negative. On occasion, if I requested, he might agree to attend preaching with me. When he did, he would put a dollar bill in the offering plate as it went by. On the way home or later at Sunday dinner, he might comment that the preacher spoke too loudly or that the building was not designed properly. That was the extent of his discussion of church.

The parent of one of my mother's kindergarten pupils told her that she and her husband were agnostics. Mom was shocked at this, apparently having never before met such a person. In my parents' religious understanding, the emphasis was on the form of religious practice. By form, I mean being baptized, attending services, being a member of the church. Nothing was ever said regarding what one truly believed or how this affected a person's life.

"I want to go up to the front of the church next Sunday at the invitation," I said to Mom. I wanted to dedicate myself to God, like others I had seen at church. Mom heard this as a request for baptism, which she viewed as something all children do at some point. Joe had done so, and now it was my turn. The whole family attended the ceremony.

Following the baptism, the church gave me a little booklet and instructed me to go over its content with my parents. Though we never discussed it, I treasured the booklet and kept it with my Bible on the shelf on the headboard of my bed, along with the small New Testament that I had received when the Gideons visited my school. Before going to sleep, I opened the Bible at random and read a few words. I never understood what it said, but it was a good thing to do.

4

A group of three girls came up to talk to me as we all waited to enter school. "Sandy really wants to make out with you," one of them said. These were the same girls who arranged for me to go steady with Sandy. In seventh grade, this was the way it was done. The whole thing intimidated me.

Junior high school opened up a whole new world. It introduced me to the world of parties at classmates' homes. Going steady meant more than allowing a classmate to wear your ID bracelet. Fellow students made out with opposite-sex partners, often uninhibited by others in the room.

Mom always dressed me in nice clothes. She even had my sweaters monogrammed with my initials on the breast. Always color-coordinated. I wore leather shoes, no sneakers. Mom admired the well-to-do class—Old Mobilians they were called—and tried to dress me as such. Once, I saw someone roll up their shirt sleeves by turning them under rather than rolling outwardly. I thought it was a good idea.

"Don't ever do that," Mom said. "That's low class." Joe and I attended private school before transferring to public school (me, grades 1-2, Joe, grades 1-7). Students wore military-style uniforms, drilling on the field and addressing teachers as Captain or Colonel. My memories of the private school are sparse. My parents said they pulled us out because of the expense. I suspected it was more than that. Mom worried we were not accepted. "His daddy is an attorney; your daddy works at the shipyard."

I signed up for band in seventh grade. Joe had played cornet during junior high, though he didn't continue into high school. Mom took me to meet with the band teacher, who asked me what instrument I wanted to play. I thought I wanted to play drums since we had a drum at home that Joe had played for the Boy Scouts.

"I want to play the trombone," I said at the last minute. Buddy and Marlene's father, Marvin Winstead, played trombone in the orchestra for events that came through town such as Holiday on Ice or the yearly Junior Miss Pageant. I sometimes saw him practice when I visited their home; the long tubular instrument fascinated me. My first trombone cost twenty-five dollars. Marvin went with us to look at the used instrument and approved it as sufficient to get started.

I took to trombone immediately. The band teacher chuckled one day as he observed me playing the required scale. I had tied a string from my index finger to the trombone slide so that I could extend it far enough to reach the required notes for the scale. The trombone has seven positions, and at age twelve, I could barely reach sixth position. This amazed my teacher, who had never before seen this string trick.

I stopped playing football after seventh grade, having tried for two years to follow in Joe's footsteps, putting on all the pads and butting heads with other players. My interest, and likely talent, lay in music. I stayed after school each day, practicing in the band room for as long as it was open. In the summer, I rode my bicycle to band practice every day.

I excelled at the trombone, received superior ratings at contests, and was first chair in the band. Granny thought I was amazing, of course, and when I played, wanted to know how I swallowed all of that tubing. I wanted a new, professional-grade trombone. We ordered one, but Daddy said to wait until Christmas. I wanted to play it for the concert in early December and talked Mom into it. Daddy never knew. On Christmas morning, I opened it as if it were my first time touching it. I played that trombone for forty years.

I always had a girlfriend, starting in third grade. Every girl I liked was going to be my wife someday. During seventh grade, Michelle was considered one of the most beautiful girls in the school. But she was off-limits since her mother was so strict. Boys who had gone to elementary school with her knew her mother was never far away, and there would never be any romance with her. We spent more and more time together after school in the band room.

I wouldn't have dared to kiss Michelle out of fear that somehow her mother might swoop in from who knows where and carry me off to some horrible punishment. Anyway, I really didn't know how to kiss. We often stood in the corner of the band room, as close as possible, my arms around her waist and hers around my neck and stared into each other's eyes. She smelled so clean, no perfume and no make-up, just beauty.

Once we went on a school field trip together. Of course, her mother went along as a chaperone. A few rows ahead of us on the bus, her mother looked back every few minutes to make sure everything was above board. Michelle asked her friend who sat in front of us to sit so her mother couldn't see through the space between the seats where we held hands.

During the summer, we wrote letters back and forth, even though our houses were no more than three miles apart. Getting together was out of the question, and her mother didn't allow her to talk to boys on the phone. We picked up where we left off when we returned to school in the fall.

I was sure Michelle would be my wife someday. A few months into the eighth grade, she sent me a note. "Let's just be friends." I hadn't seen this coming. It was my first break-up with someone I felt so deeply about.

I began to think about girls more. I hadn't remembered my feelings for Michelle being particularly sexual. But I began to be consumed with thoughts of girls' bodies. When girls went up the stairs, boys could sometimes see the straps that held up their stockings. Watching this was a common pastime. In the lunchroom, my guy friends and I surreptitiously looked to see what we might under the dresses of girls sitting at other tables.

Wanda also played in the band. She was cute, red-headed with a million freckles. She acted obsessed with me and hardly left me alone. She sometimes rode her bike to my house unannounced, came in and had a seat. She even agreed to walk up the stairs slowly so that I could look up her dress.

I spent the night at my neighborhood friend Scott's house one Saturday. He said he wanted to show me something.

"Watch. Something strange happens when I let this stream of water hit right here on my guber," Scott said as we showered together. He couldn't seem to reproduce the phenomenon for me, whatever it was, and I didn't make much of it.

Later, sort of by accident, I discovered for myself what he was talking about—beating your meat, we called it. *Oh, so that's how things work.* I felt like I had reached manhood. Sometimes Scott and I laid on the ground in the woods, dirt grinding into our bare bottoms as we engaged in this self-pleasuring. It wasn't accompanied by sexual feelings or fantasies at first, just a physical response to stimulation. I had joined a new club.

Knowledge about sex and our changing bodies came mostly from other boys and was often inaccurate. One boy in my class, older because he had failed a couple of grades, told us of his exploits with girls. We later realized his description of such things was somewhat spurious.

Mom was extremely puritanical about anything regarding the body. Joe and I weren't allowed to use words like pee, fart or pregnant. I recall being awakened abruptly one morning by Mother. She jerked my hand out of my pajama pants.

"Don't ever do that. It's nasty." What I was doing, I wasn't sure.

"Don't beat your meat too much, you could get V.D.," a friend cautioned me.

How often was too much was not clear so I endeavored to avoid the practice, with varying degrees of success. Mom would be so upset if I got V.D., whatever that was.

One classmate had a picture of a nude female that he would show you in the boy's bathroom if you paid him ten cents. One day I decided to make the investment and take a look. Just as he opened the picture and I strained my neck with the other boys to get a look at the oft-folded and creased picture, someone shouted "teacher," and he thrust the picture into his pocket, and we all pretended to be peeing.

I was at a film at church, and Wanda sat beside me. It was dark, and she didn't seem to object to me putting my hand on her knee in the darkness, even when I ventured my hand under her dress. On the way home, it hit me that I had done this in church. This was certainly a terrible sin. My heart began to pound. I trembled in fear. *God, are you going to punish me for what I did?* I tried to seek some solace from a friend.

"You tried to feel-off a girl in church?" My friend howled with laughter. I wasn't laughing. Several days passed before the guilt and fear began to subside.

I sat among several thousand teenagers at a youth rally in the large downtown auditorium.

"Some of you are born-again Christians but haven't been living a Christian life. You may have been cursing, having impure thoughts or doing impure things. You are going along with friends instead of following Jesus. Come to the front of the auditorium when the choir sings. Come and rededicate your life to Jesus Christ." Evangelist James Robison thundered forth.

Youth began to stream forward, and I joined them. I felt guilty about sometimes cursing, beating my meat or fantasizing about girls.

I had not been reading the Bible and praying. An older teenager sat and spoke with me for a few minutes, and I filled out a card. He said a prayer with me.

I'm going to live for Jesus and pray and read my Bible every day. I kept up this promise for a while, but the effort gradually diminished or disappeared completely until the next youth rally came around.

***

I was a cut-up in school. I could not resist an opportunity to make people laugh. While a good student, I was often sent to the principal for acting up. Once, I made a device that, when you sat on it and lifted up your butt, it made a farting sound.

"Does someone need to go to the bathroom?" the teacher asked the class whenever I made the sound with the fart-o-matic. She discovered it and sent me to the office with what she thought was a slingshot.

"If that happens again, there are going to be consequences." Whenever teachers said this, they offered an irresistible dare for me to do it again, whatever I had done. The bus driver banned me from riding the bus for being disrespectful. During my eighth-grade year, the band director kicked me out of the top band for acting stupid, in spite of the fact that I was one of the best players. On the one hand, I could easily feel guilty about matters that I thought my religion addressed but was willing to risk discipline to get a laugh.

5

Riot police filed into the courtyard of the school. They carried shields and wore helmets with plexiglass face guards. They carried clubs and stood in a line, every other officer facing the opposite direction. Black students stood on one side of the courtyard and White students on the other. Some of us had heard something was going on, and we came out to see what was happening. Suddenly everyone started running in every direction. A few students were hurt that day.

In 1971, I was in the tenth grade. Murphy High School was built in 1926 in the Spanish Colonial Revival style of architecture. It was laid out like a small college, the buildings resembling the Alamo. It is one of the oldest high schools in Alabama.

My parents attended Murphy in the early 1930s when it was no doubt an impressive set of buildings. No student dared walk on the grass in their day, they said. Now students hung out under the huge live oaks and smoked cigarettes before school. Paths had been worn for the shortest route between buildings.

I didn't want to go to Murphy. It was further away and involved a much longer bus ride. The previous year I had attended a more modern high school in the suburbs near our home. Because of the busing to achieve racial desegregation, I ended up at Murphy. Some families circumvented the change of schools by giving a false address. My mother tried this, but in the end, I had to change schools.

Blacks and Whites were separated by geography in Mobile. There was a small community of Blacks near where I grew up, really one street. They were poor and drove old cars that left a trail of black smoke. It wasn't uncommon to see one of them stopped at an intersection with the car's hood up, trying to get it started.

"Ain't it just like a n— to break down right in the middle of the intersection so that we can't get around," I recall someone saying. I wish I could say that I was taken aback by such a comment, but I was accustomed to this attitude.

Mom and Daddy weren't the kind of people to advocate being cruel to Blacks, or Negras as they referred to them. If Joe or I used the n-word, Mom would scold us, not because it was racist, but because it was crude. We should say Negro or Colored.

But there was no question that my parents believed that Whites and Blacks should be separate. Ironically, my mother had a photo taken in 1916 of herself as an infant in a stroller, and beside her was the Black woman who took care of her and probably nursed her from her breast. The heavy-set woman was called Aunt Page, my mother said.

Mom said when she gave birth to me and my brother, a "Colored" woman stayed with her for a period of time following each birth. I guess a Black woman rocked me during the first days of my life. I will never know her name.

The schools began to be somewhat integrated back when I was in the fifth grade. Only a few Black students lived in that school's district. The first time there was a Black boy in my class, I thought it was funny to call him Little Black Sambo. I had a good joke going until recess when he held me down and slapped my face several times. A good lesson for me.

The goal of busing was to achieve a 60-to-40 ratio (Whites to Blacks) in schools in order to match the racial demographics in the county. During my first year at Murphy, there were constant rumblings of fights or unrest. Students were required to wear an official name badge at all times.

Back in junior high, I had been a part of the crowd that was invited to the parties—sort of the popular crowd. But choosing band over sports cast me in a completely different group of people. Band members' names were not frequently called over the loudspeaker for some event or recognition. They weren't usually nominated for student council. I accepted this without regret.

After changing to Murphy, I recognized a few students with whom I had previously attended school, but they were barely visible amongst the three thousand or so students from all over the county. I had never been around Black people in a peer situation. Black male students had Afro hairstyles and carried large combs in their back pockets.

I adopted a bitter and prejudicial attitude toward them. When driving with friends, we joked that if we ran over a Black person, we earned points. I didn't think of them as people with their own thoughts and feelings. I blamed them that I had to change schools.

This was the era when students began to dress quite differently than in previous years. The transformation of student appearance had been rapid. When I started ninth grade, girls were not allowed to wear pants and boys' hair could not cover any portion of the ear.

By the time I was in high school, school administrators permitted girls to wear coordinated pantsuits. This opened the floodgates, and it wasn't long before girls wore hot pants and midriff tops. Boys grew their hair long and wore bell-bottom jeans that dragged on the ground. Colorful mismatched clothes were common, sometimes with patches about love or anti-war slogans. Old shoes or boots of some kind were common, and girls wore leather in their braided hair.

I joined in the fashion. I wore a pair of purple pants that had the faces of the crowd at Woodstock printed on them. I sported high-heel platform shoes with two-tone patent leather and silky shirts with puffy sleeves. More and more, I viewed myself as a musician and wanted to dress like it.

"You look like a vagrant. I'm taking you to get a haircut on Saturday," Daddy ranted. I let my hair grow longer, and Daddy loathed it. Mom tried to defend me by saying that this was merely the style, and all the boys were doing it.

For a while, I switched from the mod-but-clean-and-neat look to more of the hippie look. I found an old army jacket that I wore with a flowered shirt underneath it. I had a pair of bell-bottomed jeans and found a patch that said, "War is not healthy for birds or animals or humans," and sewed it near the bottom of my jeans. Facial hair was not a possibility for me yet, except for what looked like a dirty upper lip. My hair got longer and longer. I avoided Daddy.

Mom encouraged me to, at least, have some style to my long hair. She tried her best to cut my hair, so I looked like the trombone player in the band Chicago. When I went to school, girl classmates said I looked like David Cassidy, a teen idol at the time. That wasn't exactly the look I was going for.

I had a lot of albums of the music I loved. Since I played a brass instrument, I especially liked bands that used horns. I had all five albums that Chicago had produced up to the time I was in the eleventh grade. I loved Chase, a rock band headed by trumpeter Bill Chase and three other trumpet players. Their song "Get It On" topped the pop charts. I installed an eight-track tape player in my car; it protruded awkwardly from under the dashboard. I blasted the music when driving, and I got goosebumps when the trumpets squealed above the band.

I smoked cigarettes off and on, seemingly never able to fully get the hang of it. I never thought it tasted good and periodically became nauseated and threw up, always swearing them off, only to take it up again to look cool. I occasionally allowed Mom to see me smoke. After all, Joe had smoked around the house when he was a teenager. Mom smoked secretly without Daddy knowing it.

I got an afternoon job as a dishwasher at a local college cafeteria. Many workers there smoked, so I continued to try to master the skill. I looked for a brand that wasn't so harsh, that didn't make me sick.

"That's what you smokin?" another dishwasher said, laughing. The milder brand I found had flowers on the wrapper. Once, at a rehearsal of a rock band I played in, I blew cigarette smoke through my trombone for the fun of seeing it come out the end. The next day, my horn smelled like an ashtray.

"Smoothie." That was what Mr. Coleman called me. He was one of the first Black teachers I had and certainly the one who had the most positive impact on me. He was the assistant band director at Murphy. When busing of students for desegregation took place, the Black high school, Central High, closed. Mr. Coleman had been the band director at Central and held in high esteem in the Black community.

I nearly got into an altercation with a couple of Black students one day. Someone said they had tampered with my trombone. I was upset, unnecessarily. Mr. Coleman suddenly appeared. I don't remember what he said, but his presence brought calm to the situation. Over the next few years, I observed his effect on students often.

Mr. Coleman often hung a bath towel around his neck, especially when the marching band practiced outdoors in the searing Alabama heat. He constantly mopped his brow as he walked among us. He was not a strict disciplinarian, like some teachers. But you didn't want to disappoint Mr. Coleman. It was obvious he cared about every student. E. B. Coleman, as his colleagues knew him, was an accomplished composer and arranger of music. He became somewhat of a legend in Mobile.

"Mr. Coleman, can you arrange 'Back Stabbers' for us to play at the football game?" As students, we asked him to arrange popular songs we heard on the radio. Over a period of a few days, he arranged the song for band, writing out all the parts by hand. This amazed our head band director. Mr. Coleman did this in the time he had after teaching all day and working as a janitor in the evenings.

Mr. Coleman nicknamed me Smoothie because I played trombone so smoothly. I can still see his belly move up and down as he laughed, "Old Smoothie."

E. B. Coleman played in the Excelsior Band, a well-known Dixieland band, often seen marching in Mobile's Mardi Gras parades. Years after high school, I visited Mobile and attended one of the parades, and the Excelsior Band made its way down the street. Six or seven Black men marched along playing "Basin Street Blues." Among them was an aging Mr. Coleman, playing the tuba.

"Mr. Coleman," I called. When he saw me, he smiled broadly and made a motion with his hand—as if playing a trombone.

As a trombonist, I took private lessons from Mr. Thomas, considered to be the best instructor in town. He invited me to come to the church where he directed the youth choir. He wanted me to sing in the choir and play with him during an upcoming summer tour.

I drove my father's car, which was kind of sporty—a Javelin— to attend a rehearsal and decided I would do it, partly because I thought several of the girls were really cute. After we sang for the evening service, we snuck out the back and smoked cigarettes. I met a boy named Andy there. He also went to Murphy. We hung out together for a while, smoking and squealing the tires of our cars.

"If I had your car and your looks, I'd have all the ass I wanted," Andy said.

I auditioned, and they chose me to play trombone in the orchestra for a community theater production of *Oliver*. The trumpet player was really good and played in a local rock band. We jammed together after rehearsals. I went out with the cast and musicians a few times after rehearsals. My arm around one of the girls, I drank beer after beer like the others—until the waiter realized I was underage.

Marvin Winstead, Buddy and Marlene's dad, asked me if I

wanted to go with him to an invitation-only opportunity to hear Urbie Green jam with a few local musicians. Urbie Green was considered one of the premier jazz trombonists of the time and happened to be from Mobile. Marvin had played with him when they were younger.

The piano player that night was Mr. Swingle, considered to be the best in town. I knew him because I had asked him to accompany me for solo and ensemble contests and had been surprised when he agreed to do so. A diminutive man, he always looked a bit disheveled and had very little to say. Marvin said that when local musicians played for a big show such as the Junior Miss Pageant, the other musicians would see if they could get a reaction out of Mr. Swingle by slipping a picture of a nude woman between the pages of his thick book of music. When he turned the page to reveal the provocative image, he merely turned it over and continued playing, with no discernable reaction.

"Do you know Brian McDonald?" Marvin said, introducing me to Mr. Swingle.

"Oh yeah, I know Brian, he plays *a lot* of trombone," Mr. Swingle replied. That was musician-speak for a good player. My heart leaped within me.

***

David, a fellow trombone player in the Murphy band, always carried a Bible with him. He had been one of a handful of White band students the previous year when Black students were bussed in, and many White student's parents forbid them to attend Murphy High. David had long hair and a hippie look but often quoted Bible verses that explained things we were going through.

Some classmates were called Jesus freaks. They described themselves as hippies that got high on Jesus. The patches on their clothes said Jesus is the Way or Peace Comes Only Through Salvation. David added to the graffiti on the school bathroom walls writing, 'God Loves You.' Some of us questioned this practice.

David influenced me to bring a Bible to school. I started wearing a cross on a piece of leather around my neck.

I adopted the Jesus freak appearance for a period of time. But the sloppy, mismatched clothes never felt completely comfortable to me. I kept the long hair but eventually settled for less raggedy clothes. I suppose I was a Jesus freak, only a little better dressed. I followed their strict adherence to Christian behavior. No cursing, no smoking or drugs. Don't think about girls sexually—don't try to touch girls' bodies when you make out. Show love, forgive others. Close friendships should be with other Christians. Once I felt that I had gone overboard in teasing David about something.

"I apologize," I said to him.

"Don't worry. I've already forgiven you," David answered. An unusual thing to hear from a teenager.

Someone gave me a copy of *The Living Bible*. I could understand it much better than the one the Gideons had given me. I was drawn to verses that said that I was important to God, that I may be insignificant on earth, but I would be important in heaven. I underlined verses that spoke of God's concern for me. Given the seeming chaos around me, these promises reassured me.

"I left my music at home," I said. A group of band students was ready to rehearse. It was the summer after my first year at Murphy. "I don't have a car to go get it." Michael, a Black student, offered to take me to my house on his small 80cc motorcycle. Michael was like a fifty-year-old man in a teenager's body. He always dressed very neatly with a belt and leather shoes. Riding a motorcycle didn't seem to fit him.

My house was a long way from Murphy—about six miles. Michael had a helmet for himself but none for me. Since it was the law that both driver and rider wear a helmet, we got a band hat out of the uniform room, and I wore it backward, hoping it resembled a helmet.

My house was in an area of town called Cottage Hill, named so because it indeed was on top of a hill. As we made the final ascent, the little motorcycle began to labor and slowed to a crawl.

"People gonna think we are a couple of fools—salt and pepper—and you with a band hat on," Michael mumbled. It had not occurred to me that Michael riding his motorcycle through a White neighborhood with a White boy on the back might attract attention that he didn't want.

One Friday night, the marching band filed into the stadium before a football game. A couple of us noticed a White girl and a Black boy kissing in the shadows.

"Oh, gross!" someone said.

"She's kissing that?"

"His lips are the same as anyone else's," another band member said. This comment surprised me. I had never really thought much about it. I merely followed the attitudes of those around me.

My understanding of race began to slowly change. As Jesus freaks, we read in the Bible that God loved everyone and saw everyone as the same, and we embraced this. The hippie culture broke down social barriers, and this probably also played a role in my evolving views of race.

6

"Wow, Kathy and Barbara look good!" I said to the trombone player who sat next to me. I was in the eleventh grade, and it was my second year at Murphy. The two girls, both flute players, performed during half-time in the flag corps. They helped the band director hand out new music. As they put music on our stands, their long straight hair and tanned skin caught our attention. It was as if we had never seen them before.

"Look at Barbara," my friend said.

"Look at Kathy!" I said.

Kathy wore hot pants, a sleeveless top, and her long legs looked like they went on and on. She had spent many hours tanning at her family's summer home, her hair kissed by the sun. I had known her the previous year, but now she captivated my attention.

One Friday night following a football game, I asked her to ride with me to a local drive-in where a number of the band members hung out after games. She was very quiet.

"Is something the matter?" I asked.

"Does something always have to be the matter?" she replied.

A few weeks later, I stopped by her house after work from my job as a dishwasher. I was dirty and sweaty. It was mostly hormones that guided my car to her house that night. I hoped we could make out.

"Who was that long-haired boy who was here last night?" her father asked the next day.

"Why Neil, that's Kathleen McDonald's son." Her mother jumped to my defense. Some of her grandchildren had attended my mother's kindergarten, and her father knew of Mom's family growing up.

Kathy was the youngest of four children. Her sisters Brenda and Diane were thirteen and nine years older and long out of the nest. Her brother, Vincent, was three years older and started in a local college after taking a year after high school to travel with a religious singing group called Truth. He also played trombone.

Kathy's house was more modest than my family's. Her father, a fireman, had built it. The living room and dining room were one big room with a sort of wide arch between them, giving the feeling of two rooms. We didn't have a lot of privacy. We spent our time on the couch positioned in the only place in the living room where her parents couldn't easily see us.

Prior to Kathy, I had dated a couple of girls at Murphy who were in the popular crowd. Dating them was maddening since I never knew where I stood. They constantly tried to determine how they measured up in the crowd and where I fit into the picture. One day you were on, the next day off. Dating someone in the band didn't forward their aspirations for status. Kathy was down to earth, and I could tell she really liked me. I enjoyed being with her.

I began to participate in activities at my church. Occasionally I attended Kathy's church. Though much smaller in numbers, her church had a dynamic youth minister. Pastor Dave accepted me without reservation, despite my long hair and hippie look.

On Wednesday nights, we attended youth Bible study. We studied the book of Acts. Each week Pastor Dave quizzed us on what was in each chapter. The arrival of the Holy Spirit. Chapter two. The conversion of Paul. Chapter nine. Ananias and Saphira lie to the Holy Spirit. Chapter Five. I answered quicker than anyone.

"My life changed when I accepted Jesus into my life," I said in my testimony after the judo team performed at youth rallies. Pastor Dave took us to other churches to conduct youth programs for teens; the girls sang, and the boys demonstrated judo. Pastor Dave always preached, inviting other teenagers to accept Christ or rededicate their lives to Christ.

"Your breakfast is ready!" Daddy called for me from the back door of our house. I had been getting up early and sitting in the woods behind our house. Daddy always cooked breakfast. Normally the first to rise, he put on his shoes and socks and stood in the kitchen in his bathrobe and cooked. I never remember him ever being barefoot. Breakfast was always the same—eggs, bacon and toast. Occasionally, there were grits or fried potatoes if there were baked potatoes left over from the night before. Daddy must have thought it odd for a seventeen-year-old to get up at 5:30 a.m., and even stranger that I went and sat in the woods. He never asked what I was doing. I prayed. I wanted to feel close to God. "Brian," Daddy called again. "Your breakfast is getting cold."

I felt at peace in these woods where I spent so much of my childhood. Joe and I once found some vines that were strong enough that we could pretend to be Tarzan and swing from one tree to another. There was a creek where we caught tadpoles and watched them grow legs and become tiny frogs.

Not far from where I prayed was the place where I had found Gypsy two years before, lying on her side, her front legs having pawed the ground all night wearing a ridge in the earth, eyes wide with fright. Daddy was at work, and Mom was away for the day. When the veterinarian arrived, he said there was nothing he could do. He recommended putting her down. It was my decision. I walked away, heard one shot, and returned to see a small hole in her head, a crimson stream trickling out. I felt my heart rise in my throat as I stood over her, looking at her eyes, still open.

The woods were mostly silent, and the underbrush covered the paths that Gypsy had made. Each morning I read something from the well-worn Bible that I carried with me to school every day. It was small enough to fit into the breast pocket of my shirt. *God, please feel real to me.*

When I arrived at school at 7:00 a.m., I put the key in the lock and opened the door above the woodshop. Several classmates followed me into the room for prayer meeting. After reading from the Bible, we earnestly prayed that we could influence our classmates to accept Jesus, to be saved.

After school one day, I walked into the kitchen, and the mail lay on the table. On top was a clothing advertisement picturing a teenaged girl wearing a bikini. It was like a chemical reaction took place inside of me, and I went to my room to relieve the intense desire that came over me.

I had sinned again. So many times, I had vowed not to do this. A Christian friend said that masturbation was a form of lust, a sin in the Bible. "…whosoever looketh on a woman to lust after her hath committed adultery with her already in his heart" (Matthew 5:28). I prayed that I could avoid the act. I pled for forgiveness each time I succumbed. This nearly irresistible urge, and the wet dreams that sometimes occurred when I didn't engage in this self-stimulation, became a source of confusion and guilt.

If someone had explained to me that masturbation and nocturnal emissions were normal, it could have saved me a tremendous amount of distress. I believed Satan attacked me and caused me to do during sleep what I had vowed to avoid in my waking moments. Sometimes I went to sleep with my hand on a Bible passage in hopes of protecting myself from these nightly visitations of lust. ". . . [G]reater is he that is in you, than he that is in the world." (I John 4:4).

I prayed each day, multiple times. I prayed at home, even before a snack. Kathy and I prayed before going anywhere in the car, before leaving each other every day, and even when we talked on the phone. She accepted all this, never objecting. This is not to say that we didn't feel the normal urges of seventeen-year-olds. This newfound religious emphasis hadn't stopped the flow of hormones. This was tricky to handle. I was determined that we not go beyond kissing in our expressions of affection. On occasion, I became angry that we had crossed some line. I think Kathy was sometimes hurt and confused.

***

I couldn't believe it happened. They asked me to play in a real rock band, one that played for money. I dreamed of playing trombone as a professional. For a while, I had played with a band that attempted to sound like Chicago. We practiced for months, but, as is often the case, the band broke up before getting off the ground.

This band used horns as well as guitars and drums, and they opened for well-known bands when they came to town. The trumpet player I met while playing for the theatrical production of *Oliver* had recommended me.

"I'll talk to my parents and get back to you," I told the manager on the phone. He said an audition was a mere formality. There was no question in my mind that the answer was yes. My parents gave the go-ahead. Well, Mom did. Daddy didn't pay much attention.

I began to feel unsettled about accepting the offer. *What is this uncomfortable feeling?* The more I thought about it, the more uneasy I became about joining this secular rock group. *Maybe the Holy Spirit is warning me against a path that would divert me from God's will?*

I felt confused. It was an offer to do what I had dreamed of—the result of my dedication to mastering the trombone. This wasn't a garage band. The group played gigs in highly visible venues. But the more I thought about it, the more I felt that I couldn't reconcile this with my newly found identity as a Christian. The next day I called the manager.

"I set up an audition for you next Saturday . . ."

I interrupted him and said I had decided not to accept the offer. I offered no explanation.

"Where are you going with these records?" Mom asked. I had stacked all my rock albums in a pile by the door. Chicago, Blood, Sweat & Tears, Sly and the Family Stone, Santana.

"I'm throwing them away. I don't want to listen to them anymore." The albums sort of disappeared and I forgot about them. Mom took them to Dimples' house, thinking that I might want them back at some point.

I began to listen exclusively to Christian Rock. A pioneer in this genre was Andraé Crouch. His upbeat, soulful music took the religious scene by storm. By the time I finished high school, I had all of his recordings and had even attended one of his concerts.

7

"Would you like to accept Jesus Christ as your personal savior?" I said to my partner. We were in groups of two and learning how to lead someone to Christ. A college student from Auburn University held an evangelism training seminar for a number of us. It was the method used by Campus Crusade for Christ. We used a little booklet called *The Four Spiritual Laws.* "God loves you and has a wonderful plan for your life" is the first law.

As I made my way through the Bible, I noticed verses that said only those who accept Jesus will go to heaven. All others will suffer in hell—forever. "And whosoever was not found written in the book of life was cast into the lake of fire" (Revelation 20:15). *How can anyone ever be happy and enjoy life if this is what awaits the majority of people in the world, many of whom I know and love?* For months, I was so distraught about the issue of hell I could barely eat.

"What's wrong with you?" Mom asked on several occasions.

"Nothing, I'm fine," I said. What can she do about the reality of hell?

When I mentioned this to others, they said that this should motivate us to bring others to Christ. To me, the few we could convince to believe were minuscule compared with the number of people in the world. It was like trying to empty the ocean with a teaspoon.

"What about the people who haven't heard about Jesus? They shouldn't be condemned to hell for something they didn't know, should they?" I asked the pastor at Kathy's church.

"People can see from nature that there is a God. They have no excuse," he said as he showed me a verse that said as much.

"Are you saying that a person can be saved by just looking at nature and thinking that there must be some kind of creator? They wouldn't necessarily need to know about Jesus to be saved?" I asked. He looked flummoxed by this question. I slowly began to learn that if I had questions like these, I had best keep them to myself.

I browsed the religious bookstore, and among the religious trinkets, I found a wallet-sized picture of Jesus, bearded, hair to his shoulders, his face kind—a face no one could ever fear. I purchased it and put it in my wallet, so when I opened it, the first thing I saw was this compassionate face, comforting me whenever the frightening thoughts came. I focused on Jesus, not hell.

Each Saturday morning, Kathy and I went to the church around 9:00 a.m., and several of us drove to the homes of poor children and reminded them that on Sunday morning, we would come with a bus and pick them up and take them to Sunday school. I served as bus captain. Kathy sometimes went into the children's homes, often in housing projects, and helped dress them so that we could take them to church.

I kept the children occupied on the way to church by leading them in songs. "The wheels on the bus go round, round, round." My voice was hoarse, and my long hair wet with sweat by the time we arrived at church with a load of children.

Kathy and I sang in the church choir. I belted out praises to Jesus my savior. When July 4th approached, the choir began rehearsing a program that proclaimed God had especially blessed America. This felt odd to me. What did this have to do with my new life in Jesus? I went along, it was what the church did, and I was all in.

The church youth group planned a trip to perform and hold youth rallies at various churches and venues in other cities. Our judo team would put on a demonstration, and some of us would give testimonies. The girls, including Kathy, would sing, and I would be tapped to play the trombone. We were all excited. We were going to win souls to Christ.

At the end of bible study one Wednesday night, Pastor Dave said he needed to discuss something with the group. The trip would have to be canceled unless the boys cut their hair. By 1973, most boys had hair covering their ears. A couple of churches in Michigan where we planned to travel had rules about appearance. They had seen our brochure and objected to the boys' hair and the girls' short skirts.

We hardly knew how to react when told that our appearance disqualified us from sharing with others what Christ meant. Perhaps the decision to comply with this demand was harder for the boys than the girls. After all, girls could have a long dress for performances but wear their shorter skirts at other times. But for us boys, it had taken many months, even years, to grow our hair longer. In many cases, we had done so despite the protests of parents and snide remarks of other adults.

"Son, do you need some money for a haircut?"

"From the back, it's hard to tell if you are a boy or a girl."

"Brian makes a cute girl. You could call him Brianna."

We were hurt and mad, at first resisting the ultimatum. Pastor Dave had never said hair or skirt length had anything to do with the Christian life. He left it up to us whether we wanted to comply and cut our hair or cancel the trip. By this point, we had already organized fundraisers, held car washes and asked family and church members to support the trip.

"Our hair isn't really that long," one boy said.

"Oh yes, it is!" Pastor Dave shot back.

This reaction from Pastor Dave confused me. I never had any inkling that he had noticed the length of our hair. When we pressed him, he said some people viewed long hair on boys as a mark of rebellion, something inappropriate for Christians. We weren't in rebellion against anything. Besides, every picture or statue of Jesus that I had ever seen depicted him with hair down to his shoulders.

In the end, it was me who convinced the other guys to go ahead and get our hair cut. If God wanted us to go on this trip to evangelize youth to live for Jesus, then our hair was something we had to give up for God.

"Who wants to go first?" the barber said as he got up from his chair where he had been napping. As he dusted the chair with a brush, ridding it of any hair from previous customers, we sensed that he relished the opportunity to return us to what boys looked like fifteen years earlier. Indeed, when we left the barbershop that day, we resembled military recruits.

I delivered my first sermon during the trip. Pastor Dave arranged for us to present our program at the famous Pacific Garden Rescue Mission in downtown Chicago. A good place for inexperienced preachers to try their skills. The audience consisted of homeless individuals, mostly men, many of whom were alcoholics or drug addicts. Dirty, disheveled, toothless, they were required to sit through a service if they wanted to get a hot meal and a place to sleep for the night. Some dozed; others stared glassy-eyed. Not exactly the most attentive or critical listeners.

At the end of my sermon, I invited anyone who wanted to accept Christ or re-dedicate their life to Christ to walk to the front of the chapel. One man came forward. He said he had made mistakes in his life and asked God to help him through the situation he now found himself in. I prayed with him and asked God to help him. I wrote down his name and kept it on my prayer list, praying for him daily for several years.

A young Black man named Ronald, in his twenties, who worked at the mission, spoke to me after the service. He said he had been touched by my message. We agreed to keep in touch. We corresponded by mail for a year or two after that.

I felt guilty if I didn't tell every person I met about my belief in Jesus. I wrote down the names of people I witnessed to and prayed for them daily. The list became so long that I began going through it as I drove home late at night from Kathy's house, trying to get through the entire list before going to bed.

I worried about Mom, Daddy and Joe. "Have you accepted Jesus Christ as your Savior?" My questions were not always well received. "Are you sure that you would go to heaven if you died right now?" I pressed. They responded to my interrogations with something on a continuum from why sure, don't worry, to why do you keep asking me that?

My focus moved away from a future as a musician. I couldn't see myself doing anything other than telling people about Jesus. But the hard work I had put into playing the trombone stood me in good stead, and I managed to hold on to my first chair in the band, even gaining honors as first in the county and fourth in state competition. I sometimes heard testimonies of people who said they gave up things they were good at (sports, acting, etc.) in order to pursue the Christian life. I began to think of music as something I needed to give up for God.

Jeff had been a classmate for several years. Though it was a stretch to say we were friends since he played sports, wore polo shirts and Adidas shoes, and belonged to the popular crowd, he was always nice to me. Jeff participated in the Fellowship of Christian Athletes. They held a prayer meeting in the school auditorium once per week. Jeff's status and gregarious personality attracted many more students than my early morning sessions. He wanted me to play my trombone at the meetings. I felt out of place.

When some of these athletes went to area churches to give testimonies, Jeff asked me to go along to give some musical content to the program. Kathy came along with me as my piano accompanist. Prior to this, these classmates looked right through me as if I didn't exist.

One day a Black classmate invited me to come to his church to play trombone. The church was in an entirely Black section of town. Kathy's father refused to allow her to go with me, so I played the piano myself, recorded it on a tape and played along with it for the service. I asked Jeff to go with me.

"We are so happy to have Reverend Jeff with us today, and we are so happy that he has brought a friend with him," the leader of the meeting said. Jeff looked at me and chuckled in his self-effacing way. He looked older, I guess, had sideburns and the muscular build of an athlete, so they called him reverend. The congregation welcomed us.

During my senior year, the Murphy band planned to travel to the Netherlands to participate in a festival. This involved months of fundraising. We traveled to Amsterdam on a jet and spent Easter Sunday morning on the plane. I asked if I could use the empty first-class section of the airplane. I announced over the airplane PA system that anyone who desired could come and join us for an Easter sunrise service.

I led the group in singing, scripture reading, a sermon and prayer. In addition to band members who were inclined to attend, other passengers also joined the service. They must have thought it odd that a boy who hadn't even begun shaving conducted a church service.

"We are now passing over Ireland. May the resurrection of Jesus Christ bring peace to this conflict-ridden nation," the pilot announced as we flew over the British Isles. It was April 1974.

In Holland, we joked that everything cost one guilder. Hamburger—one guilder, bus ticket—one guilder. Black students in the band were somewhat of a novelty to the local people, and some walked up to them and asked to feel their hair. Freddy, a Black tuba player, stood up on the bus one day and said, "Touch my hair—one guilder!"

After returning from the Netherlands, it seemed like only a few days before the graduation ceremony. I sat on stage, in the band, wearing my cap and gown, playing "Pomp and Circumstance" as the graduates walked forward to receive their diplomas. When they began calling the names that started with the letter "M," I left the band and took my place in line. My brother Joe knelt on the floor and took a picture of me as I crossed the stage.

After the ceremony, Kathy and I boarded a bus with a group of students and headed to a prayer retreat in South Carolina. While other classmates headed out to party, we celebrated by learning how to more fully experience Christ in our lives. An aging former missionary to China, Bertha Smith, taught us how to be filled with the Holy Spirit by confessing our sins and yielding ourselves to God.

The summer after graduation involved a lot of preparation for going away to college. I worked at the commercial laundry and dry cleaners where my brother Joe worked. I had a uniform and drove a van around town, bringing clothes to and from the main plant. From the money I made, I mailed ten dollars a month to the Billy Graham evangelistic organization, responding to a plea for support during a television program.

As I drove from place to place that summer, I memorized the entire Epistle of James and could recite it, beginning at chapter one, verse one, all the way to the end, five chapters. I talked to the clerks at each of the store branches and told them how Jesus had changed my life and about my plans for the future.

Part II
Defender of the Faith

8

A bell sounded at 10:30 p.m. My roommates got up and ambled out of the room and across the hall. Boys up and down the hallway did the same. We sat cross-legged on the floor, fourteen of us in the small room. It smelled faintly of dirty clothes and feet. The bell sounded again, one minute after the first. Silence fell upon the dormitory.

Paul, our prayer captain, opened a Bible and read a few verses and made a few comments. "Are there any prayer requests?" he asked. Some asked for prayer for a family member who was sick or unsaved. Some requested prayer for a quiz the next day. "Let's pray." Someone turned off the lights, and we all knelt. We prayed, or waited, until the bell sounded at 10:45. We made our way back to our rooms. We had fifteen minutes until lights out at 11:00. This was the nightly routine in the dorm at Bob Jones University (BJU) in Greenville, South Carolina.

When Mom and Daddy dropped me off a few weeks earlier, I hadn't anticipated such a foreign environment. I visited the university with my parents and Kathy during my senior year of high school. I had not been favorably impressed. It felt stiff and cold, completely different from my religious experiences up to that point.

"Get a good education, so you won't have to work for a pip-squeak boss," Daddy had said. My parents wanted me to go to college but provided almost no guidance. Mom liked BJU.

"The students all looked so clean-cut," Mom observed.

I had heard about Bob Jones University from Pastor Dave, who had attended the college. As I prayed and sought God's will, I concluded that this was where I was supposed to go. Sometimes God leads us to do things that we don't understand. This seemed like that kind of thing. Attending any college away from home meant leaving Granny, ninety-three years old. I knew that she would probably not live for four more years. I told Granny of my reluctance to leave her to go to college.

"You have to go. You are going to bring precious souls to Jesus." Her words were a silent voice within me for many years to come. I trusted the Bible's promise:

> . . . There is no man that hath left house, or par-
> ents, or brethren, or wife, or children, for the
> kingdom of God's sake, who shall not receive
> manifold more in this present time, and in the
> world to come life everlasting (Luke 18:29–30).

Daddy had helped me take my belongings into the dorm. Mom had not been allowed to enter the male-only building. Her face twisted with suppressed emotion as she said goodbye and left me standing on the sidewalk. I didn't show any emotion. I bravely accepted God's assignment for me.

My roommates were Jay, Roger and Alan. The rooms were arranged in groups of three, with two of the rooms headed by an Assistant Prayer Captain (APC) such as mine and the third by a Prayer Captain (PC), who supervised his own room and the other two in the prayer group.

Jay, my APC, a friendly, rather happy-go-lucky junior, studied to become a high school teacher. He had a girlfriend at BJU, so much of the time during those first few days, he spent with her. Roger was a junior, too. I later learned that he wasn't an APC or PC because he had been severely disciplined the previous year when he refused to give information about some roommates who had gotten up during the night and prepared spaghetti using a popcorn popper. This incident had resulted in the discipline of a number of students. Roger had been campused, which meant he could not leave the campus for the remainder of that semester, couldn't go on weekend ministry trips, and had been stripped of any office he held.

Roger, like me, studied for the ministry. He spoke softly, had blonde hair and stood at five feet six inches tall. He kept mostly to himself. Roger navigated those first few weeks for me in this strange new place. He helped me register for classes and then, after I found out which books I needed, went with me to bulletin boards where students listed used books for sale.

My PC was Paul, a missionary kid who had grown up in India. As someone who had not been very far from Alabama, I was fascinated by Paul. He arrived a bit late for the semester and had flown by himself from India, his belongings arriving separately. While lounging in the dorm, he wore a long sari-like robe.

Each hall had a monitor. He visited each room every morning seconds after the wake-up bell rang at 6:55 a.m. to make sure everyone got out of bed. Each night the lights-out bell rang at 10:59 p.m., and we had one minute to turn off the lights and get in bed. At 11:00, the hall monitor visited each room to make sure everyone was in bed.

During the day, the hall monitor made sure that all beds were made and room duties had been completed (vacuuming, emptying trash, dusting, cleaning sink, all clothes put away, etc.). He gave us demerits for infractions. There were other duties as well. Hall monitor was a prestigious position but also one that required a lot of time.

Classes began a week after I arrived. All students had to take at least one religion class each semester. Ministerial students took two per semester. I also had to take the core courses for a liberal arts degree: History of Civilization, English Grammar and Composition, Science, and Speech.

I struggled with the long reading assignments, especially History of Civilization. Often, I spent the entire evening reading my history assignment. I managed a C the first semester. I gave priority to the religion classes, but the other subjects took time.

I often skipped lunch and breakfast in order to study. Mom was shocked at how thin I was when I returned home for winter break. Boys were required to wear ties to class until after lunch. No jeans nor shirts without a collar; always dress shoes. We had to wear a tie and suit jacket to dinner, a required sit-down meal with assigned seats. Having grown up with my mother dressing me the way she did, I adjusted easily to this.

I received a letter from Kathy that included a cassette tape with a recorded message. I went back to my dorm room, climbed up on my top bunk, put the tape in and pressed play. I had not heard Kathy's voice for nearly a month. When her voice came out of the speakers, I cried. I felt the enormity of having left everything familiar to me. The courage I had mustered for the previous weeks left me. As I listened to the tape, Jay came in and saw me crying. He smiled and left the room.

Kathy wrote to me every day. She attended a Baptist college in our hometown. We longed to be together. I also received one letter each week from Granny. Her handwriting was barely legible due to her failing eyesight. She nearly always said the same thing, "My dear grandson, I am so proud of you for preparing yourself to win souls to Jesus. I love you and miss you so much."

Mom wrote to me weekly; sometimes, Daddy wrote a few lines. Once per month, she included a receipt indicating she had deposited fifteen dollars into my account. I could go to the university business office and get cash for incidentals. I struggled to answer all these letters in addition to my studies and weekend ministry activities.

Dear God, please help me to stay close to you. I don't want to become merely academic in my faith. They encouraged everyone to have a daily quiet time, but I had difficulty finding a place to be alone and pray out loud as I liked to do. I prayed under a stairwell until I was told that I could no longer use that space. There was a study hall in each dorm where talking was not allowed, so it was good for Bible reading but not for praying, at least not the way I liked to pray.

Everything started with prayer. When I arrived at work at night, around 11:05, we assembled for prayer. Each class began with prayer. Dinner began with students standing behind their seat, and after the singing of a chorus and reading of a scripture verse, a ministerial student led in prayer.

About three weeks into the first semester was "rush" when every student was required to join a Society. I joined Theta Epsilon Chi, the same one that my roommate Jay belonged to. Societies had Greek-letter names with the exception of a few who bore the names of famous people: Bryan (William Jennings), Brönte (Emily) or Lanier (Sidney). Societies were the basis of athletic and social activities. Students held offices in their respective societies, and there was a mandatory society meeting every Wednesday.

Students could rise earlier than the 6:55 a.m. bell if they desired, but no earlier than 5:30. It was sort of a badge of honor to rise at 5:30 a.m. for personal devotions and prayer. I had applied for a work-scholarship which meant a job on campus for which I received a sub-minimum wage that was deducted from my tuition payment. I worked at night on the custodial crew after lights out until 1:00 a.m. before returning to the dorm. I erased and cleaned the chalkboards and sucked the chalk dust out of the trays under the boards using a vacuum strapped to my back in the main three-story classroom building. I straightened all the chairs. Students who worked so late were allowed to sleep through the 6:55 a.m. bell when everyone else had to get up. But if I slept much later than 7:30, I missed breakfast.

"I believe in the inspiration of the Bible, both the old and the new testaments. I believe in the creation of man by the direct act of God . . ." More than seven thousand students and faculty stood and recited the university creed as chapel began, four days per week. During this forty-minute service, there were announcements, singing of the doxology, reciting of the school creed and a sermon. Bob Jones III, the relatively new president of the university and in his thirties, or Bob Jones Jr., who was chancellor of the university, preached in chapel. Students called them Dr. Bob the Third and Dr. Bob Jr.

Their messages during the chapel service often condemned certain well-known preachers or ministries because they didn't adhere to the fundamentals of the faith or because they didn't disassociate from groups deemed to be in doctrinal error. I was taken aback to learn that even Billy Graham did not meet their biblical standard and was often the object of criticism. I continued to send Billy Graham ten dollars a month for some time after that, refusing to accept that this was not a good thing.

BJU preferred the term fundamentalist rather than conservative or evangelical. They used this designation to emphasize their orthodoxy and refused to work with others who they believed were in error. I went from being a high school kid who drew comfort from citing verses that said God knew how many hairs were on my head to a participant in a religious environment that saw itself as having an answer to every issue, from proper dress to government, from the origins of life to economic theory. These views thundered forth with absolute certainty.

9

We crowded into the lobby of the police station, twelve college-age boys in coats and ties. The government building smelled of recently waxed floors and antiseptic. There were a couple of rows of seats permanently affixed to the floor in the waiting area, a map of the county on the wall, a grimy-looking coffee pot on a corner table. A police radio crackled intermittently in the background.

All students were encouraged to go on extension on weekends. Extension consisted of some form of religious activity in an off-campus location. Ministerial students or preacher boys were required to go every weekend. On Sunday morning, three carloads of male students drove one hour north to Gaffney, South Carolina, to minister in the city jail.

"We're here to talk to the prisoners." Our leader leaned down and spoke to a deputy who slid the glass window to the side.

"Hey Johnson, the boys are here to talk to the inmates. How do you want to do this?" The officer looked sleep-deprived as he shouted to an unseen person.

"Let's put the trustees in the annex and put the rest in holding area B," answered a voice behind a wall. "Split the students between the two groups. Leave the new arrests from last night in their cells."

Six of us followed the deputy into a passageway that had bars on either side. The men, all Black, sat on benches at tables bolted to the floor. Bars stood between them and us. On one wall was a toilet with a washbasin attached.

There was an acrid smell, a mixture of cigarette smoke, body odor and general filth. On one occasion, when one of the preacher boys gave a sermon, one of the men got up, went to the toilet, dropped his pants and proceeded to have a bowel movement. The odor wafted through the room. The other inmates seemed to take no note. Most of the men assured us they were indeed Christians. It struck me that we were all White, dressed in coats and ties, and they were all Black, behind bars and dressed in jail jumpsuits.

This Sunday, it was my turn to preach. I had graduated from preaching to homeless people at a rescue mission to addressing inmates. A few of them looked up at me, many held their heads in their hands, some slept. As I preached, I stated that the God of the bible was the true God. I contrasted this with other gods that were false—such as Muhammad.

"Are you talking about the Honorable Elijah Muhammad?" one man asked as he jumped to his feet. I had no idea what he was talking about.

I later learned that Elijah Muhammad was the national leader of an organization called The Nation of Islam. Originally known as Elijah Poole, he led the organization until his death in 1975. The Nation of Islam promoted a version of Islam that emphasized those of African descent had been the original culture and that the White man had taken their culture from them.

Unlike his contemporary Martin Luther King Jr., who advocated that Blacks and Whites could co-exist equally, Elijah Muhammad believed that Blacks and Whites should be separate. Among the adherents to the Nation of Islam was Malcolm X. Young Black men who had grown up in poverty and many of whom were or had been incarcerated enthusiastically embraced Elijah Muhammad's teaching. The Nation of Islam was more than a religion. It was a political group and nationwide enterprise, operating various businesses to benefit the Black community.

My encounter in the jail took place about the time Elijah Muhammad died. At BJU, I didn't have access to secular news. We had no television and listened only to the radio station run by the university. Unless I made a special effort to read the newspaper—which as an academically struggling eighteen-year-old college student, I didn't—I knew almost nothing of news events of the day.

After preaching to the inmates, we prayed with many of them, holding their hands through the bars, leading them to recite the sinner's prayer: "Dear Jesus, I know that I am a sinner and I deserve to be punished for my sins. I invite you to come into my heart today, cleanse me from my sins, and give me eternal life." When we returned to the campus, we reported how many had been saved.

After doing this for a few months, some of us decided to follow up on the inmates who had been released from jail. Some had given us their addresses. I had never before witnessed anything like the poverty we encountered on those visits. Usually, we were unable to find the person. Those at the addresses either didn't know the person or didn't know where he was. In retrospect, two White boys wearing neckties probably aroused some apprehension.

We decided to look for a local church to pick up the responsibility for following up and discipling these men. We asked our professors and others at the university how to best find the right church for this. No one knew anything about Black churches. We contacted the only church in the same town that was ideologically consistent with the religious views of our college. We were told that Blacks were not welcome there.

Two classmates and I slid into a pew at a Black church and watched as the service commenced. We hoped to refer our Black converts to this congregation. We introduced ourselves at the appropriate time and received a rousing and warm reception of "Amen" and "Praise the Lord." It felt almost as though we were dignitaries. *Do they know anything about Bob Jones University or that it doesn't permit Blacks to attend?*

They sang louder and more earnestly than I had ever heard. There were no hymnals. "Must Jesus bear the cross alone and all the world go free," the song leader said and then the congregation sang these words. "No, there's a cross for everyone and there's a cross for me." The congregation again sang the words the song leader said.

The hymns had the same words and tune, but somehow, they sounded completely different. The fervor was palpable. The choir, dressed in beautiful gowns, swayed back and forth as they sang. As one song reached a crescendo, a woman fainted and congregants carried her out, but the singing didn't stop. Smartly dressed men extended baskets with long handles down each pew for the offering, then drew them back, moving to the next pew.

The preacher began in a normal speaking voice. The congregation punctuated his speech with "that's right," "amen," or "Oh Lord." One man with a deep, resonant bass voice added at the end of each phrase uttered by the preacher, "uh huh." Most of the time, there was an inflection that indicated agreement. But if the preacher made a particularly poignant point, his response sounded more like, "Uhhhhhhh Huhhhh" with a downward inflection as if the statement surprised the listener. The sermon proceeded in this fashion for twenty minutes. Then the preacher's voice broke into a sort of chant. "I hope you don't mind if I sing in the spirit." The congregants adjusted themselves with anticipation for what came next. Women, wearing various kinds of hats, fanned themselves as they listened, nodding in agreement. From time to time, the preacher broke from the one-note chant for a pause and sang in an arpeggio-like phrase. "Oh-oh-oh-oh-oh Lord."

This was an opportunity for the congregation to respond with their approval—"Amen" and "That's right."

The three of us were caught up in the fervor of the two-hour service. We were sure that this was a good place to encourage our new converts to attend. Mission accomplished.

The jail ministry on Sundays kept me away from campus long enough to avoid attending the BJU worship service. This was fine with me.

Female students had to wear some kind of hat to church on Sunday morning. I had seen this custom as a child in the south but had not observed it for quite a number of years, certainly not among adolescent girls. The female choir members wore hats that looked like huge envelopes perched on their heads.

Service was held in the Amphitorium, the same place where chapel was held. The more than seven thousand upholstered seats were fixed like those in a movie theater and fanned out from a huge platform—probably eighty feet across with chairs built into the wall behind it. A choir sat in an area above where the speaker of the day and a few others sat such that he—always he—could not see it. There was a grand piano at one end of the platform and an enormous organ at the other. The organ music sounded like something from a horror movie.

When it was time for the sermon, the speaker walked the distance from their wall seat to the podium, maybe thirty feet. He wore a long black robe, something that I had never seen a preacher wear. The enormous podium looked like something you might see at a political convention, wrapping around the speaker on three sides. It had the university crest engraved on the front. "Petimus Credimus—We Seek, We Trust."

The songs were not the gospel songs I knew. There was no "What a Friend We Have in Jesus" or "When the Roll is Called Up Yonder, I'll Be There." Rather, they were somber, stately hymns. "Alas and did my Savior bleed and did my Sovereign die, would he devote that sacred head for such a worm as I?" and "For all the saints who from their labors rest, who then by faith before the world confessed, Thy Name, O Jesus be forever blessed."

Prior to attending BJU, I was used to the contemporary music popular in many churches. Performing groups that came to my home church featured young adults dressed in the latest fashion, men with long hair and women in short skirts. The singers held microphones in their hands, and their bodies moved with the upbeat music. I found this exciting, and I enjoyed singing their songs.

BJU did not allow any worldly music. In fact, they explained that rock music and most popular music emphasized beats two and four rather than beats one and three. This made the music appeal to baser, unholy instincts. The dance movements such a beat naturally encouraged were not appropriate for Christians to listen to, nor should such music styles be emulated in church music.

Those who were dating could sit together, but they interacted with each other at risk of severe repercussions. Since the lights were not dimmed in church, the most you could hope for was that your legs might inadvertently brush against each other. A male student could hold the hymnal for a female student, not the other way around.

On Sunday afternoons, we went to a different auditorium for vespers. Vespers took place at 2:30 and 4:00 each Sunday, and attendance at one of the performances was required. Since we returned from jail ministry around 1:00 p.m., I couldn't get out of vespers. There were musical ensembles, readings, instrumental groups, even short plays. Each group walked onto the stage like automatons and found their spots on a riser or next to an artificial tree or other prop. *How can this be sincere? This seems too rehearsed, mechanical. How can it come from the heart?* Girls wore floor-length dresses, and boys wore suits. The people on stage stood motionless, arms at their side, only their mouths moved.

10

"Just drop it, Brian! We agree with you, but you can't fight city hall," my roommates admonished me. I had been upset by something said in chapel. Dr. Bob Jr. admonished students against not returning from the Christmas break to complete the semester. There was a significant incentive to return since a student who didn't return received no credit for the semester's work. Dr. Bob began to focus on female students who might get married during the break and not return to school.

"If you drop out of school to get married, I hope all of your children are Black." What he said after that, I didn't hear.

"We don't like what Dr. Bob said either," Jay said. Roger concurred. They tried to calm me down. I could get in big trouble if my criticism got back to the wrong people.

"It won't help to say anything about it, Brian. Just let it go!" Roger said. He looked at me with something akin to terror in his eyes.

Posted on the back of each dorm room door hung a list of rules. The last one appeared in bold print, *Griping will not be tolerated.* I began to learn what this meant. You better not say that you disagree with anything at BJU.

I found a few others who had been surprised or upset about the comment, none as much as I was. I decided to write a letter to Bob Jones III. Though not as eloquent as his father, I always enjoyed hearing him speak. Perhaps he would understand my objection to his father's comment.

I used a piece of Bob Jones University stationery and wrote out by hand my alarm at his father's comment. Barely out of high school, I had handwriting and wording that probably appeared childish. "I was taken aback at what Dr. Bob Jr. said in Chapel a few days ago. Can you please clarify for me the University's position on race?"

A few days later, I received a reply from a man who said he was executive assistant to Bob Jones III. He stated that Dr. Jones III was out of town, but he had spoken to him about my letter and had asked him to reply to me on his behalf. This assistant said it was obvious that Dr. Jones Jr.'s comments had been made in jest—that no one else had taken offense. He included a brochure printed by the university titled, "Can two walk together except they be agreed?" It was an explanation of BJU's view on separation—that believers sometimes need to separate from others who are in doctrinal error. It did not address the issue of race or interracial relations.

"It's a good Christian college, but unfortunately, it is exclusively for White Christians," Ronald, my Black friend that I met in Chicago, had written to me. His words hit me hard. *What had I done? Why had I come to Bob Jones University?*

BJU considered intermarrying of the races a violation of the scriptures and the reason Black students were not permitted to attend. BJU opposed any efforts at breaking down the boundaries God had set for mankind. In classes where this was discussed, the following scripture was cited by a professor: "From one man, he made every nation of men, that they should inhabit the whole earth, and he determined the times set for them, and the exact places where they should live" Acts 17:26 (New International Version).

I have since searched many commentaries but have never found a reputable biblical scholar who agreed that this passage says anything about race or inter-racial marriage.

"I'm leaving Bob Jones," I said to Paul, my prayer captain. "I'm transferring to another college."

"Where do you plan to go?" Paul asked.

"I'm not sure," I said. In fact, I had no idea how to change colleges. I had never considered any others.

Roger came from a family which included missionaries in Africa. He was also sensitive about the race issue but cautious about talking about it. One day he came back to the dorm and rather excitedly shared that during one of his religion classes, a few students had succeeded in getting the professor to admit that there was no biblical basis for the school's teaching against interracial marriage. That professor wasn't around for long after that.

There was talk that Tim LaHaye, a nationally known pastor and author, might come to campus to speak at the annual Bible conference. I felt proud that such a well-known person was a graduate of BJU. In the end, LaHaye didn't speak at the conference. The word around campus was that the administration was not happy with some of his associations and rescinded the invitation. Most of our speakers were graduates of Bob Jones University who conducted their ministries according to the standards and viewpoints of the institution. The famous Irish clergyman and politician Ian Paisley was a regular speaker. His bombastic voice with its Irish accent impressed me. I even asked him to sign my Bible—a practice common when a well-known preacher spoke. It was great to see Pastor Dave at the Bible conference in the spring of my first year. Former students and graduates returned for this gathering.

"How ya doin' buddy?" Pastor Dave greeted me in his normal enthusiastic manner, slapping me on the back. I hadn't seen Pastor Dave since right after the trip when I preached my first sermon. We sat together at a few of the Bible conference services. I hoped I had made him proud, attending his alma mater. He told me how many times during the past two years he had used me as an example in

his sermons to youth—how a teen in Alabama was so committed
to Christ that he was willing to cut his hair in order to serve the
Lord.

***

I threw the syllabus across the dorm room. I had vowed to sling it as far
as I could when Speech 101 was finally over in May of my first year at
BJU. Everyone hated speech, which was required of all freshmen. We
had to memorize the "Ten Principles of an Effective Speaker" from the
syllabus and write them verbatim for each exam. "The effective speaker
knows that the primary purpose of all speech is the communication of
ideas and feelings in order to get a desired response."

I watched as the syllabus fluttered to the floor like a wounded
bird. What made the class so painful was the teacher, Mrs. Harris.
Before each in-class speech, we had to sign a statement affirming
that we had practiced the speech "audibly and on your feet" a
minimum of five times. We had almost no privacy at BJU, and I
found it difficult to find a place to do this where others couldn't hear
you. The tiny practice shacks were hard to reserve since speech and
music majors had priority.

To lie was to disobey one of the ten commandments, so
you couldn't just say you practiced it aloud if you hadn't. When
a classmate hadn't fully prepared, the rest of us might have been
impressed with his improvisational skills, but Mrs. Harris didn't buy
it and gave him a failing grade.

In subsequent years, I have reflected on this class as one of the
most beneficial in my college career. Mrs. Harris, though extremely
strict, devoted herself to students and made quite an impact.

I still remember some of the things she said. In those days, it
was not uncommon for fundamentalist preachers to rail against Santa
Claus or the Easter Bunny as degradations of Christian celebrations.
Mrs. Harris had a different view.

"It is important for children to have these fantasies. This is healthy for their intellectual development," she said. Several of us glanced at each other inquisitively.

One day she talked about the power of words. She read aloud the following poem:

>Once riding in old Baltimore,
>Heart-filled, head-filled with glee,
>I saw a Baltimorean
>Keep looking straight at me.
>
>Now I was eight and very small,
>And he was no whit bigger,
>and so I smiled, but he poked out
>His tongue, and called me, "Nigger"
>
>I saw the whole of Baltimore
>From May until December;
>Of all the things that happened there
>That's all that I remember.

When hearing the poem's words, I felt like some kind of heavy darkness settled around me as if I was the only one in the room. "Nigger . . . that's all that I remember." The words were like a hot poker. I had used that word often growing up. I had avoided it after my high-school identification with Jesus freaks. But I knew it was common language where I came from. I even heard some preachers use it in conversation. I never objected. The last phrase lingered in my mind. *Of all the things that happened there, that's all that I remember.* I asked Mrs. Harris if I could copy the poem.

I later learned the poem, entitled "Incident," was written by Countee Cullen, one of the Harlem Renaissance poets during the 1920s. At the time, I knew virtually nothing about the civil rights movement and its warriors. I resolved never to hurt others with my words.

***

"Excuse me, may I talk to you for a few moments? If you were to die today, would you go to heaven?" I asked a stranger as I sat on the bench in the shopping mall.

Following my first year of college, I was required to participate in summer extension, which included witnessing to at least seven people per week. Accounts of these encounters had to be written up and mailed in each week. We also had to report participation in church activities. There were assigned readings as well.

I returned to my old job of working for Chin's Laundry. I tried to witness anyone I could find as I delivered clothing around town. Usually, by the weekend, I still lacked a few to reach the required seven, so I went to the mall and tried to talk to people who sat on the benches, often older men waiting while their wives shopped. I found this to be intrusive to them and stressful for me. But it was necessary to evangelizing the world and a part of the training God had assigned me.

"Of course, I'm a Christian. I go to church every Sunday." This was the Bible belt, and I heard many such responses. It counted toward my required seven contacts.

The teaching that all non-professing Christians were assigned to eternal punishment in hell continued to trouble me. *If this is true, why won't God enable my mind to accept it? Why does this cause me so much distress? Could it be that this is not really true? Then, what about the rest of the Bible? Jesus changed my life. I know he is real.*

I considered such doubts and questions as Satan's attacks upon my mind. I dedicated myself to preaching the gospel so that the lost could be saved. The eternal fate of non-believers was something that I would have to leave in God's hands.

Granny lived in a nursing home by then. Each day when I got off work at the laundry, I drove there and sat with her. If it wasn't too late, I fed her supper. We sang songs, and sometimes I could get her to laugh. "Remember the funny face Scott used to make?" I imitated the face. She cackled.

"Oh, you are such a good boy." She patted my hand. "I'll be in Magnolia Cemetery before long. I'm so old, I can't go on like this." I said a prayer with her before leaving for the day.

I was happy to be back with Kathy, and we saw each other nearly every day. Of course, we were involved in church together. Having been repeatedly admonished at Bob Jones to remain pure until marriage, I was determined not to succumb to the sexual urges of nineteen-year-olds. This made it hard to enjoy kissing.

Our church was affiliated with the Southern Baptist Convention, as had been my family's church. This was true of nearly all Baptist churches in town, at least the White churches. I had received a steady diet of anti-Southern Baptist teaching during my first year at Bob Jones. I learned they had been infiltrated by liberals and that obedient Christians should leave or separate from the largest protestant denomination in the nation.

BJU emphasized the inspiration and inerrancy of scripture. There could be no entertaining of the view that any single word of the sixty-six books of the Bible was in error, whether factually, historically or theologically. It didn't matter that a particular church maintained orthodox doctrinal belief. In order to be obedient to God, you must separate yourself from other orthodox believers who continue to associate with liberals. This made the community of acceptable churches quite small.

A year earlier, my church had enthusiastically sent me off to attend Bob Jones University in order to prepare for the ministry. It had graciously accepted me back for the summer and given me numerous opportunities to take part in church life. For me to be there was inconsistent with what I was being taught. I was torn as to how to handle this.

11

"You need to draw in your arm."

"I beg your pardon," I replied.

"Your arm should not be on the back of the couch as it is," the dating parlor monitor said. In no way was my arm around Kathy, but we were continually admonished to avoid the appearance of evil and not allow ourselves to be tempted.

We sat in a room the size of two basketball courts, filled with love seats positioned in every direction, coffee tables between them. One of probably one hundred and fifty couples, we sat in the Dating Parlor, the only place where we could be alone, albeit only a few feet from other couples—and the watchful eye of the monitor.

It was my sophomore year at BJU, and Kathy joined me. The previous year when we were at separate colleges, Kathy explored the possibility of attending Bob Jones University. Her parents were not keen on this, but when Kathy makes up her mind to do something, she is not easily deterred.

"I guess there is nothing I can say. You seemed to have it all worked out," her father said when she showed him her figures of how it would be paid for. We could be together only in certain places such as the snack shop, dating parlor or a sanctioned event on the campus. Someone was always watching. The best we could hope for was that our legs might touch, something for which we would be reprimanded if observed. Nonetheless, we enjoyed many happy hours in the dating parlor.

The "dating outing" was an anticipated activity each year. Each society sponsored an activity during the fall or spring to which one could invite a member of the opposite sex for a picnic-like gathering somewhere away from the campus. Girls could invite a boy to their outing, and boys could do likewise to theirs.

Kathy and I enjoyed a picnic lunch followed by various games and skits. All the girls wore culottes. Kathy wore my Theta Epsilon Chi jersey with "Brian" stitched on the back. Her hair braided into two pigtails, she looked adorable. To someone happening upon the scene, we must have looked like the cast of an old movie. We were allowed to hold hands while playing couple soccer. This was the first flesh-to-flesh contact Kathy and I had experienced since the previous summer. A few jocks got a little carried away and dragged their dates behind them as they chased the ball.

On the thirty-minute bus ride back to campus, I looked out of the bus window as we bounced along. The world looked so different, only a short distance from the campus—houses filled with people, children at play, people who likely didn't hold the pure beliefs that we did. I looked down at a car next to us and thought about the people inside. *Are these people saved or are they headed for hell?*

The bus turned into the beautifully manicured campus. Ahead was the amphitorium with the BJU emblem emblazoned on its façade. My mind went to the daily chapel services when all of these students and faculty recited the university creed. *Yes, this is the true way, it must be, so many people agree.* I pushed the doubts to the back of my mind.

***

"Ahm Brine McDonul from Moooobil AAAAAlabamer." The other players mocked my accent when the members of the trombone choir introduced themselves. Even though the school was in South Carolina, most of the students were from the northeast, mid-west or west coast, so my heavy drawl was a novelty to them. I took it in stride.

I started playing in the university trombone choir. I loved this group, about twenty-five trombone players and a few euphoniums and tuba players. Many of the best players majored in music. We performed at vespers several times a year; always a favorite of students. In order to participate in any ensemble at the university, students were required to study with an instrumental instructor and practice five hours per week. I even appeared playing trombone on BJU's television broadcast a couple of times.

It was somewhat of an anomaly for a fundamentalist institution to have such a premier musical group. BJU was all about high culture. We had to attend Shakespearean plays, Italian operas and view ancient art, especially of a religious nature. The university housed one of the largest collections of religious art in the US. Attendance at all of these programs was required.

The trombone choir played classical music by composers such as Wagner, Ravel and Bach, and also religious music of the high church genre. Our conductor had studied at the Eastman School of Music. I was the only non-music major who played in the elite Trombone Octet.

**

It was ten o'clock in the evening, and boys stood in the lobby of the dorm where I lived. Some were in gym shorts, others in pajamas, some still dressed as they had been for the day. We waited for the campus mail. Two male students came running in, panting, carrying a wooden box with dividers separating letters for the four male dorms. They dumped the contents of the section for our dorm, and we converged on the letters. Most envelopes had the first name of a male student with the dorm name and room number written under it (Bill, Graves 224).

Some eagerly awaited a girl's response to their letter the previous night asking to meet for lunch or go to church and vespers together on Sunday. A guy pumped a fist in the air as he opened the letter and learned that his invitation had been accepted. Another crumpled the note. "Shot down again."

Some envelopes, like the one I looked for, had two names and two dorm addresses; for people like Kathy and me, who exchanged letters each evening. Brian, Reveal 231 / Kathy, Mack 328. We reused the same envelope night after night.

Kathy and I knew each other's schedules and arranged to walk together to classes as much as possible. We met in front of the post office or in front of the dining common. If we attended a concert together, and it was dark, Kathy hooked her leg under my leg, and this mild intimacy could escape notice. We were never allowed to be away from campus together unless we secured a chaperone. I think we did that once for a double date, but it was awkward, and we never did it again.

***

"Mr. McDonald, please come to the board and write the verb conjugation for Aorist Active Indicative, using the verb, *Agapao*," my Greek instructor called on me. I did so confidently, a feeling of pride pulsing through my veins.

In my second year, I took Greek and found that I loved it. Many preacher boys dreaded this subject; many struggled with it, a few flunked it. Some had to change their major from Bible, which required Greek to something else like Church Administration, which could also qualify one to be a ministerial student but didn't have the Greek requirement.

I had squeaked by with Cs and a few Bs during my first year. During my second year, I applied myself to Greek with all my determination, fearing I would not be able to hack it. I was determined to pass it even if it meant slighting other subjects.

I carried vocabulary cards with me everywhere I went. I reviewed verb conjugations constantly, glancing at them as I vacuumed the hallways of the dorm late at night. I became one of the top students in the sophomore class. My overall confidence grew, and the discipline that I gained in this ancient language spilled over into other classes. I made the dean's list every subsequent semester of college.

I took other Bible classes and became increasingly versed not only in scripture but also in the fundamentalist approach to understanding and applying it. I pushed away troubling thoughts of the eternally damned. I focused instead on the mercy and love of God. There was a plan to save people from eternal punishment.

Kathy always took a lot of the teaching with a grain of salt. Perhaps because she was not a ministerial student, or due to her personality, she simply didn't seem to be so taken with all of the rigid viewpoints.

Some students became interested in Calvinism. This was not the official view of BJU but was often discussed. This approach to theology (sometimes called reformed theology) emphasized that God is in control of everything, that nothing happens unless God has ordained it to happen. God has chosen certain individuals to be saved. The theological term for this is election. These individuals are predestined to be saved and others to be lost. Given my ongoing struggle around the issue of eternal damnation, I found it particularly terrifying to suggest that God may have actually chosen certain people, apparently many people, for eternal damnation.

A few students and maybe a few professors adhered to another view that emphasized the free will of human beings. This was called Arminian theology. But this view argued that after choosing Christ and being saved, one could conceivably fall from grace by committing certain sins or denying Christ, and thus again be lost and not make it to heaven.

Some ministerial students enjoyed debating these two views. I found it to be much more than an interesting topic. On the one hand, the concept that once a person was saved, they could never again be lost no matter what, the Calvinistic view appealed to me. But, the corollary teaching that God chose who would be saved in the first place repulsed me. I wanted to believe that every person had an opportunity to choose to believe and thus be saved.

I walked out of the classroom building, and Kathy was waiting for me to walk to lunch together. Wearing one of the below-the-knee skirts that her mother had made the previous summer, she held her books against her breast with both arms. My heart leaped a bit when I saw her.

We walked together toward the dining common (we weren't supposed to be together unless we had a legitimate reason to be going to the same place). She looked at the notepad on top of her books, where she had listed things to talk to me about. I called her notepad her "dwelling place of all generations." She was already thinking about the approaching Christmas break and was telling me her plans.

Back home for Christmas break, I wanted to bring Granny home from the nursing home for a few hours on Christmas day. A nurse had helped her into her best dress and put her hair up with pins. Not exactly like she usually wore it, but she looked nice.

Granny could no longer walk. I carried her in my arms like a baby. She had always been a small woman, and I suspected she weighed no more than fifty pounds. "Oh, what a beautiful bow," she said as she unwrapped each of her gifts. She carefully folded the wrapping paper, putting it aside for future use. She eyed her growing stack of presents with satisfaction.

She didn't speak during the ride back to the nursing home. I sang hymns, "Rock of Ages," "The Old Rugged Cross." She joined in, feebly.

***

"Brian, call your mother," the note on my dorm room door said. It had been only a few weeks since returning to BJU after the holidays.

"Granny is gone," Mom said.

I suppose that Granny's passing left a huge hole in my life, but that isn't entirely accurate. More than forty-five years later, I can still see her in my mind's eye as clearly as if she were right in front of me, her snow-white hair in a bun, her toothless laugh, her wrinkled hands marked with age spots. *Oh, you're such a good boy.* I had heard her say it so often. I know it sounds trite, but I really do feel her with me.

Granny was born in 1880 when Rutherford B. Hayes was president of the United States. Her father fought in the Civil War. Through her stories, she connected me with a time long past, a time when automobiles had not yet been invented, when medical care was primitive, and many children (including her) were orphans because their parents died of diseases now rare or easily curable.

As arrogant as it may sound to say it, I knew she adored me. To have been loved in such a manner was an immeasurable gift.

12

I squeezed my way around other students to get to my mailbox in the campus post office. I reached over someone and turned the dial to open it. We checked our mailboxes several times per week. A professor asked for a student conference or the business office requested payment of fees. Report cards or a letter from home.

A letter from the pastor of a small church in my hometown arrived. I had met him briefly during the past summer and learned he also had attended Bob Jones University. His church was not Baptist but was called a Bible Church; quite small with thirty to forty people. Kathy and I visited there a couple of times. At one service we attended, there was no pianist, so they asked Kathy to play.

Pastor Bertram wrote inviting me to come and work for the church during the upcoming summer to help evangelize the neighborhood and serve as an assistant to him. He would give me opportunities to preach and participate in other ministerial duties. The church proposed a salary of one hundred dollars per week but could not afford to pay me weekly. Instead, they planned to contribute one hundred dollars per month to my tuition.

Ministerial students were encouraged to have some kind of summer church work. The previous summer, I had gone back to my job at the laundry. Earlier that spring semester, I interviewed with the director of Neighborhood Bible Time. The preacher boys who went with this group often took commercial airlines from place to place. They memorized a few prepared sermons and were coached to deliver them smoothly and dynamically. I knew some of these students who were often finalists in the yearly sermon contests at BJU. A rather high-profile summer activity. Traveling with this evangelistic group could be a real feather in my hat.

The opportunity in my hometown appealed to me in a different way. The opportunity to prepare my own sermons, preach and be near Kathy and my parents. I decided to take the position with the church in Mobile.

The trombone choir was invited to perform at the prestigious International Trombone Association Workshop held right after the spring semester ended. Many of the leading trombonists, both classical and jazz, would perform at the festival and players from all over the country would attend. When school let out in May, I traveled to Nashville with the trombone choir. The director wanted someone to be a chaplain for the trip, and since I was a preacher boy, he chose me. Whenever the group gathered to warm up for a performance or to plan the next day's activities, I first brought a devotional message. I still enjoyed playing trombone, but I focused more on pursuing my future as a preacher. I left the festival early to assume my summer ministry position.

Pastor Bertram was a gentle, soft-spoken man. He came from Pennsylvania, and you couldn't imagine two more different pronunciations of American English than his and mine. He always looked a bit disheveled and carried a few books with him everywhere he went. Wherever Pastor Bertram and I went—to visit the elderly or those in the hospital—he stopped by the religious bookstore and browsed. On one occasion, we rode together to visit an elderly person, and he became distracted by our conversation. Without realizing it, he pulled up in front of the religious bookstore.

Pastor Bertram was the exact opposite of the flashy salesman-like preachers who often preached at BJU. He was easy to talk to, unassuming and loved to read books and discuss them. He genuinely wanted to give me opportunities that were beneficial to me, not just those that lightened his load.

I wore a tie and walked from house to house in the sweltering summer heat of Alabama. "Are you certain that if you died today, you would go to heaven?" I asked any person who opened a door. "Would you like to know how you can be sure that you would go to heaven?" I invited each person to church and left them with some literature.

I worked in Vacation Bible School, dressing up like a clown, playing my trombone to entertain the children. I occasionally had opportunities to teach Sunday school or preach during a worship service. Pastor Bertram encouraged me to read commentaries and books to help me with my sermons. I felt more like a preacher. I also mowed the church lawn. The church was set on a three-acre lot, so this was a never-ending task.

Kathy came to the services on Wednesday and Sunday. Her family wasn't happy that she no longer attended their Baptist church. Mom came if I had some role in the service. My brother's wife sometimes attended and brought their six children. Eventually, my mother and brother's wife became regulars at the church.

During my conversations with Pastor Bertram, I discovered that he adhered to the basic tenets of Calvinism. *Oh no, not this again.* I had never heard Pastor Bertram say anything to this effect in any of his sermons, and when he and I visited people together, he always encouraged them to accept Jesus as savior.

"This is just the way the scripture reads to me. But I'm trying to do everything I can to bring everyone to salvation," he assured me. I reasoned that as long as he wanted every person to be saved, then his professed adherence to Calvinistic theology was not an issue for me.

***

"I found out what I want to do! I want to be a linguist. I want to be a Bible translator," I said to Kathy when we met to walk to class. I had heard a presentation at the start of our junior year about individuals who go to remote parts of the world and study the languages of people with whom no one has ever been able to communicate. The ultimate goal was to be able to share Jesus Christ with them.

Due to the difficulty of such a task, some Bible translators were considered the best linguists in the world. I had discovered that learning Greek, something the majority of ministerial students hated, was something I loved and grasped easily. *Yes, this will be the way that I will use my unique ability in the world.*

I ordered books on the subject. Kathy shared my excitement. This required extensive graduate education. We dreamed about the future and moving to some remote part of the world.

But as time went on, this dream faded. I didn't know how to pursue something so different from what my classmates did. Also, it felt a little too much like a pursuit of something for me, something that made me feel good about myself. *Is this pride? If it makes me feel so good, can it be what God wants?*

My classmates elected me to be chaplain of my Society. At each meeting, I gave a brief message. I rejected any nominations for positions such as president or vice-president, preferring to serve only in the spiritual leadership roles.

***

I looked up at the stage from where I sat in the orchestra pit. I could hear the singers but could only see them when they approached the edge of the stage. I played in the orchestra for a production of the opera *Fidelio*. The composer, Beethoven, didn't write an extensive part for trombone. None of the trombone majors wanted to do it since the time investment was large, but the actual playing time was limited. I jumped at the chance.

There were long sections of the opera where I didn't play at all. The conductor didn't care if you read or studied during those times since the audience couldn't see the orchestra. During rehearsals, students who majored in voice understudied the major roles. The university music department always arranged for one or two singers from the New York Metropolitan Opera to take the leading roles. At the dress rehearsal, when the real singers stepped in, they stunned me with the power of their voices. On one occasion, I missed my entrance. The conductor gave me the evil eye. I avoided this happening during any of the actual performances.

***

I received a call slip in my campus mailbox that said to go to the office of the Director of Ministerial Training.

"Your mother called, and she thinks that the site of your ministerial practicum is too far away. She doesn't want you to drive that far," Dr. Stenholm said. I felt a sick feeling in the pit of my stomach.

The ministerial training department assigned me to do my third-year internship at a church in High Point, North Carolina—more than a three-hour drive from Greenville, South Carolina. I could drive the used car I had purchased the previous summer.

Here it was again, my mother's overprotectiveness. As a teenager, Mom interrogated me if I wanted to go somewhere with friends. Once, my friend Andy called and wanted me to go somewhere with him. I stood in the kitchen with the phone in my hand.

"Ask him what time you will be back," Mom said.

"Tell her you'll be there when you get there," Andy said to me, thinking my mother couldn't hear. She heard.

"Oh yeah, then you won't go at all!" she had said.

"I have been supervising preacher boys for twenty-five years and there has never been an accident. Whenever there has been any kind of car problems, God has always sent someone along to help," Dr. Stenholm told my mother. He had experience with parents. "You have nothing to worry about," he assured her. What could she say?

For an entire semester, I drove the three hours to High Point with three other preacher boys. We left on Saturday mornings, did church work all weekend, and returned to the BJU Campus late Sunday evening, usually after midnight.

The fundamentalist churches where preacher boys interned were White congregations. I observed that racial prejudice was not necessarily considered un-Christian. The pastor of the church where I interned was a nice enough man. But he didn't hesitate to use the n-word.

BJU had recently relented and allowed a few Black students to enroll. The pastor commented that one of the few Black students had become quite visible at BJU, his picture often appearing in publications.

"You can't treat a N…. like that," the pastor said. He suggested it was a mistake to place Blacks in leadership or highly visible roles. I didn't say anything. Having struggled to overcome my racism during high school, I encountered it as an acceptable attitude in the company I kept. I am ashamed that I didn't have the courage then to stand up for what I believed.

Each evening after supper, I attended Missionary Prayer Band, a fellowship that met for the purpose of praying for missionaries. When I visited the group designated "Far East," I saw a poster that stated this part of the world comprised one-fourth of the world's population but had the fewest missionaries. China had not allowed missionaries since the communist revolution in 1949. We read the letters of the missionaries in Hong Kong, Singapore, Korea, Taiwan and Japan.

Missionary Prayer Band cut into my study time, but I felt guilty if I didn't attend. We knelt and prayed earnestly that people in these faraway places be saved.

Kathy and I talked about our future. We wanted to become instruments in God's service. We chose II Chronicles 14:11 as our life verse as a couple: ". . . Lord, it is nothing with thee to help, whether with many, or with them that have no power: help us, O Lord our God; for we rest on thee, and in thy name, we go against this multitude. O Lord, thou art our God; let no man prevail against thee."

After returning home for the holidays, I stopped by Kathy's house when I knew she wasn't there to ask her parents for their daughter's hand in marriage.

"How about a foot?" Kathy's father said, always the jokester.

I purchased an engagement ring with the help of a BJU faculty member who sold jewelry on the side. I used pretty much all the money I had saved up to that point, around nine hundred dollars.

"Will you marry me?"

Kathy looked stunned. I guess she hadn't guessed this was coming after all. Her eyes became misty and she struggled catch her breath. "Yes, of course."

We had dated for more than four years. We had discussed this possibility often. We planned to marry the following December 1977.

Fiancée. Returning to school after the holidays, I felt great using this word to refer to Kathy.

That spring, a missionary family we had become familiar with visited the campus. An announcement was made that students interested in this ministry could meet with them. Kathy and I stopped by and talked with Mrs. Faust, an elderly woman who had gone to Taiwan in her sixties, and her adopted Chinese son, Boya.

Kathy was open to becoming missionaries together since, as a child, she had been involved in a Baptist youth group, Girls Auxiliary, that emphasized missionary work. We talked about it often during our time sitting in the dating parlor.

Boya Faust took a picture of Kathy and me. We didn't think much of it. Later we saw that he printed the picture in their newsletter with the headline, "God has chosen them for Taiwan." *Is this God's way of telling us?*

I saw my academic studies as part of my spiritual life. Previously, I tried to have a devotional life separate and different from academic study of the Bible, but now when I studied Greek or Systematic Theology, I believed this expressed my devotion to God as much as having my daily quiet time.

I rarely read anything but the Bible or Bible commentaries. Pastor Bertram encouraged me to read other books, but I feared this might lure me away from the Bible. My high school education had not been rigorous, and I struggled with college assignments that required extensive reading.

***

The summer following my junior year, I again assisted Pastor Bertram, engaging in various duties of the small church. I preached more often. Our wedding was to be in December of that year, so Kathy spent much of the summer arranging all the details. Before we returned to BJU in August, she had everything ready, including her wedding gown, which she designed, and her mother made. She had scheduled the photographer, florist, cake, everything.

13

We started classes in the fall of 1977. I could hardly believe our marriage was a mere three months away. *I'll be sitting in this very seat as a married man before this semester is over.*

Kathy and I signed up for a class together, American Family, taught by a faculty member who emphasized the importance of establishing a *Christian* family. We dreamed and planned together how we wanted our home to be a thoroughly Christian place where we prayed, read the Bible, participated in church activities and reared our children to be committed Christians.

August through December crept along. One or two other classmates had gotten married the previous summer, but most were still single. Since sex is reserved for marriage, those who had wed possessed a wiser, more mature aura, having experienced this mysterious longed-for act. No one ever discussed it. Together, Kathy and I read a book called *The Act of Marriage* by Tim LaHaye. Ok, we knew what to do and were very excited about it.

Kathy and I met each evening after dinner, and I walked her to her dorm slowly as we talked about the events of the day and our approaching wedding. The line of couples walking from the dining hall to the girls' dorms was nicknamed the Snail Trail because couples walked as slowly as possible, squeezing out every possible moment together.

The wedding was to be on December 17, 1977, the day following our arrival home for Christmas break, also my twenty-second birthday. We traveled to Mobile a few weeks before the wedding to apply for the marriage license in person. License secured, we set out on the nine-hour drive back to Greenville to finish the remaining few weeks before the wedding.

I drove, and Kathy laid her head on my lap to sleep. This closeness, knowing that we would, at last, be able to satisfy our sexual desires in just a matter of days, stimulated me sexually. Kathy noticed my arousal and touched the moisture that appeared on my pants. It was a tender moment. After all, we were on the home stretch, and nothing had really happened that was wrong. But the episode, rather than excite me, frightened me.

It wasn't as though something like this had never happened during our five years of dating. We had explored each other's bodies early on in high school, always vowing to avoid doing so after becoming religiously committed. But now, we were just weeks away from marriage. This was too close. What if Kathy got pregnant and a baby came eight months into marriage? This wasn't going to happen. I knew how intercourse worked and how a woman became pregnant. But my mind was set into a spin with this terrifying thought.

The devastating effects of violating the sexual standards of the Bible had been emphasized often and strongly at Bob Jones University. This sin had ruined the lives of many a preacher.

"Be careful of the rustle of skirts . . ." one speaker had said.

Avoid any possible temptation. Do not close the door when a woman is in your office. When visiting church members or prospects, if a woman is the only one at home, do not enter the house. Such warnings were common.

What if Kathy becomes pregnant by coming into contact with my semen while lying in my lap, somehow it finds its way into her vagina while using the restroom? This was absurd, I knew. But was it impossible? What if that happened? But we haven't had sex!

As we continued the journey, and the fearful thought came to me, I dispelled it as ridiculous, almost laughable. I was embarrassed to tell Kathy what was going through my mind. But the intrusive thought kept returning. When it did, my heart pounded, and a feeling of terror came over me. One of the biggest events of my life—my wedding—was about to take place and while on one level I was very excited and happy, on another level, I was terrified.

Those last few weeks before the Christmas vacation were so anxiety-filled that I could only limp through my studies. I sought relief from scripture. "Who shall separate us from the love of Christ . . .? For I am persuaded that neither death, nor life, nor angels, nor principalities, nor powers, nor things present, nor things to come, nor height, nor depth, nor any other creature shall be able to separate us from the love of God, which is in Christ Jesus our Lord" (Romans 8:35, 38–39).

Pastor Bertram performed our wedding ceremony in the little church where I had served the two previous summers. The ceremony started about thirty minutes late because people were trying to get into the narrow driveway and into the church. Kathy and I had prepared a little printed scroll to be given to each person.

> *The Psalmist exclaimed: "I love the lord be-*
> *cause He hath heard my voice my supplica-*
> *tions." There are no better words to express our*
> *feeling as we come to this special occasion in*
> *our lives. We love the Lord because of what He*
> *has done for us. The Apostle John expressed*
> *the same thought as he said, "We love Him*
> *because He first loved us." Our love to God is*
> *only in response to His greater love which was*
> *manifested in the giving of His Son to die for us*
> *on the cross. Such love deserves more than we*
> *could ever give in return. Our desire today, as*
> *our lives are united is that, together, we might*

*bring praise to the one who gave His very life
for us. The one thing needed to make our joy
complete on this occasion is to know that each
of you also knows and loves our wonderful Savior. May God bless you.*

Kathy and Brian
December 17, 1977

After the reception, we set off on the two-hour journey to
Destin, Florida, where we honeymooned. My aunt and uncle let us
stay in their condo near the ocean. It was cold and rainy. We found
one boat that agreed to take us deep-sea fishing, but on the appointed
day, the weather was too rough, and the trip was canceled. Our first
intimacy didn't exactly have the seamless flow that movies suggest.
It took a few days to get the hang of it, but it was worth the wait.

The circumstances that had triggered the anxiety passed, but
the feeling of dread—that something bad was going to happen—
didn't go away.

We enjoyed our time together but were eager to get back to
Greenville and move into our home. After a shorter honeymoon than
planned, we returned to Mobile and, after a brief visit with family as
a married couple, set off for our new home.

Part III
Grown Up

14

I carried Kathy across the threshold of our new home, like in the movies. The apartment was part of a church fellowship building in a rather seedy part of town. The rent was sixty dollars per month and reduced further if we cleaned the small church twice a month. The building had four apartments, one of which the church used for Sunday school rooms. Les, also a ministerial student, and his wife Starry were about our age and lived in one of the upstairs apartments. They were expecting their first child. Two male students lived in the other upstairs apartment. Each apartment had three rooms accessible by a hallway. It had not been originally built as apartments, so the floor plan was odd.

We had a small dining area in the rear of the apartment with a tiny kitchen behind that. The refrigerator had a small freezer compartment that held a couple of ice trays and a few items. It frequently froze over until it became impossible to get the trays or food out. Once a month, we had to unplug the refrigerator, place a pot of hot water inside and allow the frost to melt, sopping up the water with towels.

The bathroom had an old claw-foot tub, large enough to stretch out in with water up to your neck. We had a second bathroom with a shower, something the other tenants didn't have. Our kitchen opened to the back driveway of the church. A common front door opened into a foyer, and the four apartments were accessible from there.

The sign on the building said Parish Hall. Sometimes people knocked at the door asking for food or money. Kathy fixed them a sandwich, and I witnessed to them, inviting them to accept Christ as savior. Occasionally I gave them money, but friends cautioned us against this, lest they come more often. On occasion, I gave them a ride somewhere in my car, to the local rescue mission or the Salvation Army.

The two male students who lived upstairs worked odd hours, sometimes returning home during the middle of the night. One night, one of them came in the front door and found a homeless man asleep on the floor.

"What are you doing here? You can't sleep here." After that, we made sure that the front door stayed locked.

The windows were of the vintage type that had weights in the wall that helped you raise the heavy paned units. When the wind blew, the windows rattled in their casings. A few times during the night, I imagined someone knocking on the window asking to come in. We wedged pieces of cardboard into the window tracks.

We enjoyed our long-delayed sexual relationship. We wanted to wait to have children at least until I finished my master's degree. Kathy really wanted to teach for a couple of years. A local church-run school had already offered her a position to teach first grade after graduation.

We decided to use condoms for birth control. While I still lived in the dormitory before the wedding, I had purchased condoms. I felt extremely nervous as I walked up to the pharmacy counter. "Excuse me, sir. Could you tell me where I can find this?" I handed the pharmacist a piece of paper with the name of a particular brand of condom. Pastor Bertram had advised me that the best condoms to use were those made of lambskin. Very natural. I waited for a response from the pharmacist, who adjusted his glasses and looked at the slip of paper. *Does he suspect I am a BJU student? I have the identifying short hair and necktie.*

"Aisle nine," he said and returned to his work.

They weren't cheap—fifty cents per condom. We had very little money, and this was not an insignificant amount, especially given the frequency with which we planned to put them to use. Sweet Kathy, ever thrifty and excited about our recently enhanced relationship, rinsed them out and hung them in the bathroom to dry and re-use. I was skeptical, but it was all new to us, and we were happy.

Next door was a beautiful old house with a big porch across the front. At one time, it had been the office of a chiropractor with a dwelling above it. The sign was still there, but the building had fallen into disrepair. Dr. Fowler still lived there. I sometimes found him lying in the driveway, unable to get back into the house. I helped him get up on several occasions. He smelled of alcohol, sweat and urine. When sober, he was a well-spoken, intelligent man who enjoyed conversing. He had a German shepherd named Girl who was always there to receive him when I got him into the house. He never mentioned my assisting him in this manner. Perhaps he didn't remember.

I got a job as assistant manager at the campus bookstore, where the other students now had to call me Mr. McDonald. Just like that, I was an adult with a wife, an apartment and people calling me mister. I took a couple of classes the previous summer to lighten my load for the one remaining semester after the wedding.

Kathy still had a full load of classes. We happily began our married life in this way. We could buy a pound of chicken livers for a dollar. We got two meals out of this. We loved our little home.

On weekends, we traveled to a small town about one hour away, where an older classmate served as the pastor of a small church. I taught a class or organized activities for the teenagers. Kathy and I drove up early one Saturday, and along with a few other parents of the teens, we took them to an amusement park called Carowinds. The weather looked threatening. Thunderstorms can come up with very little notice in South Carolina. Before I could even plan for shelter, the skies opened, and rain came down in buckets.

I hurried the group of twelve- to seventeen-year-olds into the nearest building to get out of the deluge. A show was about to begin. Great timing. It was an old west can-can show where women danced and held up their skirts to reveal colorful underpants. *Oh boy, this isn't good. Women dancing, holding up their dresses.* The church didn't allow girls to wear pants and their dresses and culottes had to be below the knee. We walked out of the theater into the bright sunshine—the storm having passed.

"Brother McDonald, I dunno 'bout you, but I sho got my eyes full," one of the adult male chaperones whispered to me.

We traveled to the church each weekend. We didn't have money to eat out following the service and counted on families to invite us to Sunday dinner. Some of these congregants became like family as we began to find our way as a couple.

We became close to one family with four children, ranging from one in college at BJU to a five-year-old. The older children played guitar, banjo and sometimes mandolin. They regularly performed at church, singing southern gospel songs. Each Sunday afternoon, the boys played their instruments and sang, their eight-year-old sister standing in front of them belting out the words. I dreamed of someday having a family who could do this.

We planned to stay in South Carolina for two more years while I pursued a master's degree. Some students set off for the ministry after receiving a bachelor's degree, but I didn't feel ready.

***

We sat in the examining room of the university clinic. A young female nurse sat across from us, holding a file folder. She delivered the positive results from the rabbit test.

"I am pretty sure when I got pregnant. I remember the night the condom broke." Kathy said. I winced slightly, probably blushing.

This wasn't part of the plan. The nurse looked at us inquisitively, trying to discern whether we were happy about this news.

The lambskin condoms may have been natural but apparently not reliable. On the night of the malfunction, Kathy frantically filled the tub full of water and sat in it.

"Go to the drug store and buy a douche kit," she had said.

"A what?"

"A douche kit. Ask someone, hurry!"

We had not signed up for the health insurance that included maternity and childbirth. In order to pay for medical expenses, I took an extra job delivering newspapers, and Kathy worked in a local doctor's office until the baby came. Kathy and I watched with wonder as her tummy began to swell. We had hardly gotten used to saying wife and husband, and now we were going to be parents.

We received our bachelor's degrees in May 1978. Both of our families came. Everyone congratulated us on our graduation and on the news that we would soon be parents.

15

It became harder for me to devote time to my spiritual life. The responsibilities of schoolwork, two jobs, ministry on weekends, and a baby on the way put more demands on my time.

We attended pre-natal classes. Couples sat in a circle on the floor. "My pantyhose won't stay up now that my stomach is so big," one expectant mother said. The soon-to-be fathers, all BJU students or faculty, looked at each other with embarrassed expressions. In October 1978, a few months prior to the birth of our baby, we attended natural childbirth classes. The men practiced coaching their wives through contractions.

Since we didn't have family nearby, the people in the country church we attended on weekends, as well as the other employees at the campus store, encouraged and guided us. *What if Kathy goes into labor and I am off on my paper route and she can't get in touch with me?* I rented a pager with a number that would cause the pager to sound if called. I would know to get to a payphone and call or get home right away.

In graduate school, I delved deeper into the complexity of the faith that I had embraced as an adolescent. We plowed through the three big volumes of *Hodge's Systematic Theology*. I learned how the beliefs that I took as accepted doctrine had been debated for centuries. Arguments for the existence of God or the nature of human beings—body, soul and spirit, or just body and soul—resulted in various sects and denominations.

We studied liberal theological and neo-orthodox views only to refute them. Is hell a literal place? What is paradise? Is there an afterlife? Will we know people in heaven? While we might read differing views, if a student actually embraced a position not in line with the university and our professors, the student was considered to be in doctrinal error.

Occasionally doubts crept into my mind as to whether hell existed, where all who had not accepted Jesus as savior would spend eternity. Was hell a real place or a symbol of something else? When Jesus spoke of hell, he often used the word *Gehenna*, which actually referred to a garbage dump on the outskirts of Jerusalem, continually smoldering as refuse burned. It may have been reasonable to conclude it was a metaphor, but no one dared embrace this view. Hell, as a literal place, seemed to be an essential component of fundamentalism.

Entertaining such thoughts brought into question many other teachings of the Christian faith. Was God really three parts: father, son and Holy Spirit? Did the supernatural events recorded in the Bible really happen or were these just myths passed down by Jesus' followers?

I quickly expelled these thoughts as satanic attempts to rob me of my faith. "...the devil, as a roaring lion walketh about, seeking whom he may devour" (I Peter 5:8–9).

***

On Thanksgiving Day, the newspapers were large and heavy and had to be delivered in the morning rather than the afternoon. Seven months pregnant, Kathy insisted on going with me to help. She sat in the back seat and folded the nearly two hundred papers, put rubber bands on them and put them in plastic bags. This way, I could finish quicker, and we could be home for our first Thanksgiving as a couple.

"Stop the car, stop the car!" Kathy said. I pulled over to the side of the road and watched as she opened the car door to throw up.

On January 18, 1979, Kathy gave birth to a baby boy. The birth had not been easy. He apparently inherited genes for a large head both from me—always had difficulty finding a hat that fit me—and Kathy's father. Stuck in the birth canal for some time, he finally emerged with the help of forceps.

"Is his head always going to look like that?" I asked.

"It will round out," the doctor assured me.

We named him Brian Rush McDonald Jr. in the southern family tradition. A new life had been added to our union. Les and Starry, who lived above us, already had a baby girl born only a few months before.

"Hey, come on up, we have ice cream!" Les yelled down the stairwell. Happy times. Going to the laundromat to wash diapers was time-consuming. Les suggested we purchase a washing machine. We made monthly payments to a local department store. We installed the washer in the bathroom in the church fellowship hall. This way, both families had access to it whenever needed.

"Make sure to put the drain hose in the toilet when you wash," I reminded the wives. Kathy hung the diapers on a clothesline in the driveway outside our apartment. We believed that God had given us our son. We prayed that we could rear him so that he would live a life that glorifies God. We cited the scripture, "Lo, Children are an heritage of the LORD .... As arrows are in the hand of a mighty man; so are the children of the youth. . . ." (Psalms 127:3–4)

I sat in front of the choir loft in a small orchestra in the sanctuary of a church near Atlanta, Georgia. I had agreed to play trombone for an Easter cantata. I thought it would be a nice outing for Kathy and me with our new baby. And it involved a little pay. Kathy and I made the two-and-a-half-hour drive from Greenville and planned to drive back late that night after the program.

"Brian! Brian!" Kathy screamed. She came running into the sanctuary and thrust Brian Rush into my arms. His little face appeared to be scraped and bruised. *What is happening?*

Kathy had taken him to the nursery to let him nap while I rehearsed. When he was asleep, she walked back to the sanctuary to listen to the choir and orchestra. When she returned to check on him, he was not in the crib where she had left him. She couldn't imagine where he was.

She had noticed a little boy run past her as she approached the nursery but didn't think much of it. Finding Brian Rush missing from the crib, she began frantically looking for him. She heard a sound coming from the adjacent bathroom.

The little boy apparently tried to pick up Brian Rush, and when the infant cried, he tried to stuff him in the toilet. Thankfully, his head was not under water. There were scuff marks on his face from the boy's shoes.

My heart nearly pounded out of my chest. I felt I might vomit. Kathy cried hysterically. I took Brian Rush in my arms and looked around at the stunned faces of choir and orchestra members. Someone called for an ambulance.

The police arrived first. The Black officer seemed like a huge angel as he cradled Brian Rush in his arms, awaiting the ambulance. Kathy sobbed uncontrollably. A choir member tried to console her.

Kathy and I stayed at the hospital with Brian Rush for five days, sleeping together on a chair that pulled out to make a one-person cot. Each day we waited nervously as a pediatric neurologist examined our two-month-old baby. When the doctor came, he held up a mobile of a bumblebee that hung over the crib. Brian Rush's little eyes followed as the doctor moved the bright toy across his line of vision. For several days, his eyes followed the toy to the halfway point of his field of vision and stopped there.

On the fourth day, Brian Rush's tiny eyes followed the toy all the way across. We cheered with joy at this breakthrough. The neurologist determined he had suffered a slight skull fracture but with no apparent lasting consequences. The boy at the church eventually confessed to what he had done.

God, are you trying to tell me something? Have I become too academic in my approach to my faith and future ministry? I thought of times when I was inwardly dismissive of the preachers I heard who didn't really expound the scriptures as I was learning to do. I didn't want to think that God allowed this to happen. *God, from now on, I'll attend every service with an open heart and listen to every sermon and allow you to teach me from the lips of your servant, no matter who it is.*

***

We moved to a little four-room house a mile from the BJU campus. No more than five hundred square feet, it had two small bedrooms connected by a tiny bathroom. When you entered, there was a living room with a small kitchen off to the right. It had a floor furnace between the kitchen and bedroom. No air-conditioning. A door led out of the kitchen to the side of the house, and another door off the living room opened onto a small porch. No back door. The house badly needed painting, and the landlord agreed to pay me to do it. I worked on it steadily, puttying all the windows, scraping the house and painting it.

I came home from work each night to a prepared meal we ate sitting in the little kitchen. Brian Rush had started to crawl, and we feared he might burn himself on the floor furnace. Kathy's daddy found a kind of barrier that stood over the furnace to keep him off it. We loved our little house on Essex Court.

At 4:00 a.m., I brought Kathy a cup of coffee and told her that it was time to wake up. I took a class that had a paper due every Friday at 9:00 a.m. Kathy was a much better typist, and she agreed to type up what I'd stayed up late to write. She sipped the coffee, rubbed her eyes and stretched.

"Don't you dare wake the baby," Kathy whispered sternly. The new Smith Corona electric typewriter my parents had given us made it much easier. If you made a mistake, you could switch to the correction cartridge, type over the mistake, re-insert the ribbon cartridge and type it correctly. While somewhat quieter than an old manual typewriter, it still made noise, and we weren't far from the adjacent nursery where Brian Rush slept. We tiptoed and whispered. I fixed some breakfast while she typed. If she was fast, maybe she could catch a little sleep before the baby awakened.

I looked admiringly at the row of commentaries and theological books that I had collected for my future ministry. Once when Brian Rush pulled some of the books off the shelf, I scolded him. At that moment, I had an insight. This little creature was a human being distinct from me, not something to be controlled. He had a mind of his own, and his life was to be respected, loved and nurtured.

***

I neared completion of my master's degree. Brian Rush was now sixteen months old. Kathy and I cleaned another church each Saturday to help with our bills. We socialized with a few other couples, but other than our former neighbors, Les and Starry, we were the only couple with a baby. We were all so strapped for money that when one of the couples invited us to their apartment for a get-together, they figured up the total cost for charcoal, drinks and meat and asked us to cover our portion of the expense. Kathy got a job cleaning a house that was full of antiques. She set up a playpen, and Brian Rush slept or watched as she tooled around with a dust cloth.

We immersed ourselves in the religious and social views of Bob Jones University. Current events were either unknown by us or analyzed, criticized or refuted by our teachers and preachers we heard. The university had its own radio station. The only music played was classical music or the high church style of sacred music that BJU sanctioned. Occasionally Kathy tuned the radio to the local public radio station. It played classical music, so it should be safe to listen to. There were a few other news programs on that station in addition to the music, and consequently, it gave us a peek into a different approach to news and world events.

Late one night, I sat on our bed and listened to the denim voice of President Jimmy Carter. He tried to be reassuring, but things were not good. He had ordered an attempt to rescue the fifty-two US citizens who had been held hostage by revolutionaries in Iran. It was the spring of 1980, and the standoff between the US and this heretofore little-known Middle East country had dominated the news for months.

President Carter explained the situation. The mission had not been successful. In fact, it had gone terribly wrong, and eight US service members were dead. As I listened to him, it felt like nothing was going right for the US or for President Carter.

I marched in graduation ceremonies in May 1980 but needed a couple more summer courses before officially getting my master's degree in September. At twenty-four, I had been in school my entire life. It was time to begin a career. I believed God had called me to the ministry, but I wasn't sure exactly what that was going to look like. I had a wife, a son and another baby on the way. I needed a job.

16

If someone had asked me to name as many US states as possible, I would likely have forgotten Kansas. But here we were, in Newton, a city of 18,000 people in the middle of wheat country with a grain elevator in every little town. Most of the people were of German descent with names like Schmidt, Unruh or Brunner. Newton sat at a crossroads of the Santa Fe and the Missouri Pacific railroads.

A few months earlier, I had given my name to the university ministerial placement office, indicating I was willing to serve as assistant pastor somewhere in the southeastern US. There were a few inquiries, but nothing worked out.

As fall approached, I had to leave my job at the campus store because I was no longer a student. I worked as a waiter in a restaurant for a brief time. Had we planned for a second child? Sort of, I guess. But given that I was on the verge of becoming an unemployed ex-student, it certainly wasn't wise.

In late August, I received a call from a pastor in Kansas. How they got my name, I'm not sure. Things moved quickly. Kathy and I made a weekend trip, during which time I taught Sunday school, spoke to the youth group, rehearsed and directed a choir performance, preached a sermon and attended a deacons meeting. If we accepted the position, I would be Assistant Pastor in charge of Youth and Music.

They offered the position, and I accepted. We returned to Greenville and packed up our things. My parents bought us a newer used car, an AMC Hornet. Kathy was seven months pregnant. With the car packed to overflowing and Brian Rush sitting between us, our little family made its way from South Carolina to Kansas. God's plan for us unfolded.

I had my own office, with a desk, swivel chair and bookshelf. My two degrees hung on the wall. I even had my own bathroom. (Well, it had previously been the baby nursery, so there was a sink and toilet in an adjacent room.) Finally, I got paid for what I had set my mind to do as a career. I had my Bible open on my desk and a commentary beside it, preparing to teach Sunday school. The phone rang. My boss was out, so I answered.

"Meridian Baptist Church, this is Pastor Brian." I loved my new moniker.

"Pastor, this is Bethel Deaconess Hospital calling. We have one of your members in the hospital and wanted to notify you." In this town, everyone belonged to some church and when checking in to the hospital were asked to indicate which one. "Mrs. Kathleen McDonald is in room 314," she said.

This I already knew. The night before, November 3, 1980, Kathy had given birth to a girl, Margaret Rebekah McDonald.

Sunday came around less than a week after Margaret was born. As the weekend approached, Pastor Jerry began to mention to me that some mothers missed church after the birth of a child.

"There is no reason to miss church because you have a baby." He said that the good families brought the mother and child to church the first Sunday after the birth. Pastor Jerry and his wife had two children; they were both adopted.

"I'm not ready to go to church," Kathy said, barely five days after giving birth. Kathy has always been a no-nonsense person. My boss met me with a look of consternation when I arrived at church on Sunday with only Brian Rush in tow, no wife and no new baby.

We settled Margaret into her nursery, one of the three bedrooms in our apartment. Three bedrooms and two baths were almost unbelievable. Our apartment, while low-income housing, was by far the nicest we had ever lived in. Most of what we had in the way of furniture had been donated or loaned to us by church members.

Kathy did not work outside the home. However, she was expected to participate in everything I did. When I was hired, the contract stipulated that Kathy type the weekly church bulletin and play the piano in church as needed.

The bulletin involved typing on a mimeograph stencil. It had to be typed on Saturday so that last-minute changes or announcements could be included. It usually only took a couple of hours, but for a mother of a toddler and an infant, it was a two-person job since she couldn't be distracted lest she makes a mistake. My job was to ride herd on the children. After she typed it, I took the stencil to the church and put it on the drum of the mimeograph machine, cranking the handle and watching the machine spit out the bulletins, ink still wet.

Church members hovered around and supported us. Our children eventually called one older couple Maw Maw and Paw Paw. Others they called Aunt and Uncle. I settled into my duties, including directing the choir. I accompanied Pastor Jerry to visit prospects each week and alternated with him visiting those in the hospital. There was a lot to do, but I was happy to be here.

***

The local Newton High Schoolers were the Railroaders. Tracks ran diagonally through town, and you could be delayed for a long time by a passing train. There was a huge antique locomotive in the town square. Our license plates were royal blue with a golden shock of wheat.

"Are you from Oklahoma?" someone asked when hearing my drawl.

The first big youth event I organized was called a Hobo Happening. Fundamentalist churches rejected the themes of witches and ghosts for Halloween. The idea of hobo came to me in a book about youth ministry.

Toward the end of the Sunday worship service prior to the event, a dirty, disheveled-looking man wandered into the sanctuary. People looked around at each other, not knowing exactly how to react.

"Is this the Hobo Happening?" the unshaven man asked. I had asked Orville Brunner, a church member and engineer with the Santa Fe Railroad, to dress up like an old hobo. He played the role convincingly. A number of members were rather stunned until they realized it was a stunt.

The event happened on a member's farm, where we had various hobo-related activities: a bonfire, hobo stew, a hayride, and roasted marshmallows. The church's old bus rattled and creaked up in front of the barn, and forty or more teenagers spilled out. I suppose having a new youth pastor in a small town generated a lot of enthusiasm. The turnout surprised and pleased Pastor Jerry.

"I hope you have a good gospel message to preach to all these kids. A lot of them need to be saved," he admonished me as I rallied my adult helpers to start the first activity.

***

I opened the church door, and as I did, I saw the headlights of Sam's car. At 5:30 a.m., the church was dark and silent. Sam, a church member about my age, met with me one morning each week to pray together. I had a stack of 3 x 5 cards. On each was the name of a teenager.

We knelt on the floor of my office, going through the cards one by one, praying they would be saved and, if already saved, be completely committed to Jesus Christ. When we were through praying, Sam left to go to his job at the city water department, and I started my day at the church.

My relationship with Pastor Bertram back in Mobile had been so comfortable. Being around Pastor Jerry felt different. He was a bit of a curmudgeon and had an opinion, a strong one, about many things. If a young person had long hair, he said it looked shaggy. A man with facial hair looked rather wooly. He learned that we had bought disposable diapers for a sightseeing outing and feigned humor as he told the church about it during a sermon. You would have thought he had caught us in an evil act. He and his wife had never used disposable diapers, he said. No matter that they hadn't been invented when his children were babies.

Pastor Jerry and the deacons decided to launch a ministry to the senior citizens of the church. I was now in charge of the youth, the music and seniors.

I named the group the Prime-Timers. These senior adults had time and enthusiasm, and they weren't hard to please. Having grown up with Granny prepared me to feel at ease with them. Kathy helped, and they looked upon us as their grandchildren. The Prime Timers brought us pastries and vegetables from their gardens. One elderly couple who also served as custodians at the church brought us fresh eggs each week. We had a monthly luncheon and occasionally went on outings.

Once, I planned a three-day-long trip for the Prime Timers to Eureka Springs, Arkansas, to see the famous Passion Play. I drove a fifteen-passenger van through the winding roads of southern Missouri into Arkansas. My head throbbed by the time we arrived. I wanted nothing more than to hit the sack. I assumed a group of senior citizens were also tired and did not want to get up early the next morning.

"Would it be alright with everyone if we met in the lobby in the morning at 7:30 a.m.?" I asked.

"What's wrong with 6:30?" one piped up.

There was less of an expectation to evangelize the senior adults. They all came from some Christian background—many in that part of Kansas had grown up as Mennonites. I was expected mainly to show love and care for them. That I felt comfortable doing.

"If you are a pastor and you don't win at least one new person to Christ every week and get that person to come to church and walk forward during the invitation, you should be ashamed to pick up your paycheck." These words came from a speaker at an evangelism conference I attended. Wow, I needed to step up my game.

I planned into my weekly schedule a time to go from house to house looking for individuals who I could lead to Christ. I utilized a rehearsed approach I had learned at the conference, asking them to repeat the sinner's prayer after me. I suppressed the feeling that I was being manipulative and disrespectful to these individuals with the smooth salesman-like approach.

Only one individual ever came to church and walked forward at the end of the service as a result of these door-to-door efforts. He never came back, though I visited him often and urged him to return. One person at whose home I had left some gospel literature wrote me a letter. He believed that if one was not baptized in water, then they could not be saved and thus would go to hell. He challenged me to a public debate on the topic, and I initially agreed, but at the urging of church members who knew the individual, I pulled out.

For religious holidays, such as Christmas and Easter, I put on a musical program. The choir practiced several selections or a cantata. The problem of a pianist limited our musical selection. Kathy could play hymns well but could not play the intricate accompaniments of most of the choir arrangements. The same was true of the dear lady who also played piano on occasion.

One of the firm opinions of Pastor Jerry was that a church should never pay an outsider to play in the church. Such a person might not share all of our beliefs and might not adhere to our standards. He had a strong opinion regarding the music I selected for the choir. On the one hand, it couldn't be the least bit toe-tapping, nor could it have any contemporary flavor. On the other hand, he said he didn't want any long-haired music, by which he meant classical or High-Church sounding music (e.g., Brahms, Bach). It was a fine line to negotiate.

He was leery of organ music lest it sound too staid or stuffy, though we had an organ, and his wife was the organist. "I love the sound of a Hammond organ. I wish we could get one of those," he often said. I knew what he meant.

"You mean one of those organs that they play at the roller-skating rink?" I asked.

"Yeah, I guess that is the kind they play there, isn't it?" he said sheepishly.

***

I straightened my tie and checked myself in the mirror. My hair was neatly trimmed, revealing skin above my ears. I wore a three-piece suit, my pocket-watch chain attached to a button, the lowest vest button intentionally left unbuttoned. I walked into the church sanctuary where eight other Baptist ministers sat, including Pastor Jerry, for my ordination examination.

It was customary to convene a group of pastors from like-minded churches to examine a candidate for ordination. I had been in the ministry full-time for almost a year by the summer of 1981. In my hand, I held a copy of a doctrinal statement I had prepared, covering all the orthodox doctrines, with scripture references to support each tenet. I had gone over and over it.

The pastors perused their copies—Soteriology (doctrine of salvation), Hamartiology (doctrine of sin), Pneumatology (doctrine of the Holy Spirit), Ecclesiology (doctrine of the church), etc. Each section had a point, followed by a sub-point, followed by another sub-point, and so on. *I hope the questioning isn't too long and grueling.* I felt somewhat nervous. Mainly, I was ready to get it over with.

A current hot issue among conservatives was the charismatic movement that had swept through many churches, both evangelical and mainstream, during the past decade. This movement advocated the practice of speaking in tongues. Pastors struggled with whether or not to accept this practice.

"You have to address the issue of tongues in your doctrinal statement," Pastor Jerry had urged me. "They will need to know that you are solid in this area." He meant I needed to show opposition to the practice of speaking in tongues. This was difficult because there really was no prohibition of the practice in the Bible. In fact, quite the contrary.

As I prepared my statement, I included a few scripture passages that, while not specifically forbidding the practice, at least cast some doubt on the modern practices. Some pastors believed the following verse addressed the issue: "But when that which is perfect is come then that which is in part shall be done away" (I Corinthians 13:10).

Several verses earlier in this chapter referred to "speaking with the tongues of men and of angels" and having the "gift of prophesy." These are two of the gifts often associated with the charismatic movement. Those who felt this addressed the speaking-in-tongues issue believed the phrase "that which is perfect" referred to the canon of scripture we now have. In other words, when the Bible was completed, there was no more need for speaking in tongues and prophesizing.

From my own study of commentaries on the passage, I concluded that the words "that which is perfect" likely referred not to the Bible but to Christ, the "perfect one." I felt it was a misapplication of the passage to assert that it forbade speaking in tongues in the current era. While I personally had not experienced speaking in tongues, I was not inclined to manufacture a biblical prohibition of the practice.

"You didn't include the passage from First Corinthians 13 that shows tongues are no longer operative in the present age," Pastor Jerry noted as he reviewed my statement. He had no doubt this passage clearly taught that speaking in tongues should no longer be practiced.

"I am not sure that verse addresses the issue of tongues today," I said. "I have searched a number of commentaries on the matter."

"You need to study that some more," he responded without hesitation. In other words, his interpretation of that verse was the correct one, and I should include it. What was I to do? I reluctantly included the verses. In the end, this issue didn't come up during the questioning.

"Could Jesus have sinned when he was tempted?" one of the ministers asked during my examination. This question surprised me, not because I had never heard it before, but because I didn't expect that any of these men would entertain such a question, a question I viewed as silly.

"Oh," I said, sort of shrugging. "Is that a trick question?" I sort of grinned. I really didn't think the questioner was serious. Pastor Jerry didn't like my response. He stood and addressed me as one might a confused child.

"Is Jesus God?" he asked me in front of the other pastors.

"Yes, of course," I answered.

"Can God sin?" he continued.

"No, he can't," I said.

"There you go," he said. I didn't respond further.

The actual ceremony took place a few days later on a Sunday when the church deacons laid their hands on me to ordain me to the ministry. My parents came for the event.

"If this newly ordained minister ever ceases to believe the teachings that he has affirmed today," Pastor Jerry said to the congregation as I stood before them, "then he should return this ordination certificate to this church." Now, I could write Rev. before my name.

Each day as I prayed, I thanked God for allowing me to find my way into the true faith, the Old Time Religion, as I often heard preachers call it. Those in most other denominations were liberals and not on the straight and narrow path, I believed.

17

"You are going to have that baby soon, I just know it," said a lady in line behind Kathy at the grocery store. Kathy was buying Karo syrup to make a pecan pie. "I wanted pecan pie just before having one of my babies," the lady said.

Kathy went into labor that night. Daniel Harris McDonald was born on November 9, 1982. His hair was black like Karo syrup and just as greasy.

"A lot of people are adopting those little Indian babies," an elderly woman said when she saw Daniel with his jet-black hair.

We were a family of five now. I tried having a garden to raise vegetables and even bought a bunch of chickens for one dollar each and asked an older member in the church to help me kill and dress them. The meat was too tough to eat. We ended up boiling one once in a while and giving it to our dog Fella. The garden attracted insects I never knew existed.

When I dug my potatoes, they were the size of golf balls. Fella sniffed each disapprovingly. Fella was Margaret's nemesis, jumping up and licking her mouth, hoping to find a morsel of food. The little mongrel had the maddening habit of darting out the front door if he saw it ajar. After chasing him around the neighborhood a few times, I concluded that he would return when he was ready, not before.

"Brian, there's a phone call for you," Kathy called from the back door.

"Who is it?' I asked.

"It's Pastor Wilson," she said.

Pastor Wilson had taken the place of Pastor Bertram when he moved to another church in a different city. I knew him but couldn't imagine why he was calling me. We exchanged pleasantries.

"The church members felt that you should know that Pastor Bertram has had a nervous breakdown," he said. *A nervous breakdown?* He didn't offer any explanation of what this meant, and I really didn't know what to say. Nervous breakdown was the term Mom had used to describe what had happened to Daddy.

"Oh, my goodness. How is he?" I asked. Pastor Wilson said Pastor Bertram had resigned from the church where he was pastor and was receiving some kind of treatment. I thanked him for the call and hung up the phone.

I stood in our little kitchen and began to cry. I had not cried like this since I was a child. I wasn't sure why I was crying. It just felt like some kind of lifeline had been severed.

When I had some big event planned for the church, the anxiety returned, like in the early days of my marriage. I feared many things. I claimed every promise from the Bible that I could. *Is this my "thorn in the flesh" as the apostle Paul talked about? God's grace will be sufficient for me. (II Corinthians 12:9)*

***

"Can you paint?" the voice on the other end of the line asked me.

"What?" I said. I didn't recognize the voice.

"Your ad said odd jobs. Can you paint?" The voice sounded like an old man. Money was scarce, and I tried various ways to make extra cash. Sometimes the local funeral home asked me to sing for a funeral. There had to be a soloist for every funeral in Newton, Kansas. I could slip in the back door after the service had already started, stand out of sight behind a screen, point to the hymn in the organist's hymnal, sing "Amazing Grace" or "The Old Rugged

Cross," and leave. I earned fifteen dollars for every performance. They were good gigs; there just weren't enough of them.

I had forgotten about the ad I had placed in the local paper a few weeks prior, "Will do odd jobs." Who can't paint? It was a farm way out in the country. The farmer looked ancient, and his equipment looked like it belonged on *Green Acres*. I had to climb up high on a wobbly ladder to paint the peak of the barn.

"More often, not as deep," the old farmer yelled up to me. The oil-based paint ran down into my armpits. I painted on Mondays, and it took a week to get it all off before doing it again the next Monday. I guess he thought I got more on me than on the barn. "More often, but not as deep!" he yelled up to me again. He thought I dipped the brush too deep into the bucket.

"The paper is in the can!" his wife yelled out the back door as I walked down the path to the outhouse. I'm sure the house had indoor plumbing, but I wasn't allowed inside.

"I love you so much. I hope this day away from your normal responsibilities is good for you." Kathy had tucked a note inside the lunch she had packed for me one Monday. I sat in the shade and enjoyed my lunch, thinking about her, Brian Rush, Margaret and little Daniel at home waiting for me to return.

We depended on the generosity of our family and church members. Up to this point, every car I had owned had been purchased by my parents or with their financial help. Whenever they came to visit, we hoped they might offer to buy something that we needed.

Pastor Jerry equated frugality with godliness. As I worked for him, I began to see a pattern that explained some things that happened early on. Back when they interviewed me for the position, he said the church could not afford a plane ticket for Kathy to accompany me. Given the active role a minister's spouse is expected to play in the work, this perplexed me. My colleagues at the campus bookstore had taken up a collection to purchase Kathy's ticket.

When we moved to Kansas, he said it would be difficult for the church to pay for a moving truck. He asked us to pack our belongings in boxes and instructed us to give them to various people who were returning to the Kansas area after dropping off their children at BJU. In the end, a church member who was in Greenville to drop off his daughter saw our belongings and told Pastor Jerry the plan was not feasible. Pastor Jerry acted like the amount of stuff we had after less than three years of marriage was excessive.

Pastor Jerry forbade any discussion of the church purchasing a van for use with the youth ministry. Renting a van was out of the question. I had to ask members to volunteer to drive several cars in a caravan.

"We praise the Lord for His faithfulness and for laying it on the hearts of our members to give generously to pay off this mortgage many years before scheduled." Pastor Jerry beamed as he addressed the congregation. The church held an event when the building mortgage had been completely paid off. Everyone clapped as Pastor Jerry set fire to the church mortgage and dropped it into a trash can.

Each year the church had surplus income and put it toward paying off the mortgage. Was this what members intended when giving? I didn't know. *Why do we have to struggle so much when the church seems financially healthy? I'll never get myself into another situation where I don't have enough to provide for my family and have no way to rectify the situation.*

Mom and Daddy purchased us a bigger car since we now had three children; a little station wagon with four doors. We now had two car seats in the back and an infant seat in the front between us as we went to church on Sunday—about the only place we all went together.

We didn't participate in any activities other than those of the church, and church members were our only friends. We didn't know anyone else, and our strict religious associations discouraged participation in many activities. Association with unsaved people further than casual encounters was only to evangelize them. To be fair, we had wonderful friends among church members, people who cared deeply for us.

If we wanted to go out for dinner without the children, we went through the church directory and considered the advisability of asking each family to watch the children for a few hours. Always, we had to take into account how it might look for me as one of their pastors to ask them for this favor. Had we asked this person before? How long ago was it? We couldn't afford to pay a babysitter and didn't know one to ask anyway.

We were a long way from family. I wasn't really happy with my role and my boss. What about our prior commitment to becoming foreign missionaries? *Lord, is this your way of nudging us to move forward to the next step?*

18

The highway in western Kansas went on and on ahead of us with very little change in scenery. Grain elevators marked the little towns we saw off in the distance. There were wheat fields all around us. Our little station wagon was packed and had a luggage carrier on top.

Kathy was on her knees, leaning over the seat feeding Daniel, now six months old. Brian Rush and Margaret sat in car seats on either side of him. It was May 1983, and we were on our way to Colorado to begin "deputation."

The previous fall, we had decided on the next step in our lives, the part we were to play in God's plan for the world. We planned to become missionaries.

The meeting with Pastor Jerry earlier in the year had been stressful. I proposed a Sunday or Wednesday off now and then to visit other churches to seek financial support for my family for our missionary plans. His brow furrowed as it often did when he was nervous or annoyed. I had been there more than two and a half years, and things had gone pretty well. He had hoped I'd stay longer.

We planned to begin official deputation—the seeking of financial support—full time during the summer of 1983. Since I didn't have a salary, we hoped a few churches would already support us monthly by then.

Aspiring missionaries travel from church to church, put on a program and share plans to go abroad. The goal was for churches to put us in their budget for a portion of the support we needed to live in another country. We felt sure the church in Newton would have a financial part in this. The people loved us, and although Pastor Jerry had not been the easiest to work for, we nonetheless respected each other.

The raising of financial support and living on what we received along the way proved to be more difficult than we imagined. We were young and idealistic. Our families and other more seasoned church members scratched their heads, wondering how we were going to manage to stay afloat. "God will take care of us," we said. We anticipated this process taking a year, hoping to leave for our intended destination in 1984.

Had it not been for Kathy's gung-ho and pioneering attitude, we wouldn't have made it. Her family didn't have much money as she grew up; they taught her how to make a lot out of a little. We didn't have any money when we got married, and now, three children later, that had not changed.

Since we weren't affiliated with a denomination that could underwrite our financial support, we applied to a mission board. This organization certified the missionary was in agreement with a doctrinal statement and became a clearinghouse for financial support. The mission board provided some logistical help, though this was largely left to the individual missionary to work out.

We looked into several fundamentalist mission boards whose missionaries our church already supported. Most of them were Baptist. As rigid as I had become in my beliefs, I was still not inclined to have the label Baptist at the forefront of my ministry. We decided to apply to the mission board affiliated with Bob Jones University.

A few years earlier, we had met Boya and Mrs. Faust, who had encouraged us to consider Taiwan for our future ministry. We trusted God knew what he was doing.

We faced the task of introducing potential supporters to a country about which we had no personal knowledge. We acquired some slides from missionaries who were already there and put together a presentation. Kathy and I rehearsed a couple of duets using my guitar as accompaniment. I prepared a trombone solo or two. We tried to make our presentations entertaining, and our children always accompanied us so that people could see a family planning to move to another country to reach the lost for Christ.

We visited two or three churches each week during the month in Colorado. We often arrived at a church, usually the evening before a presentation, not knowing where we were going to stay. The church pastor usually asked a church family to host us, or sometimes we stayed with the pastor's family. All of the people we encountered were so kind and gracious.

Occasionally a church had converted one of the church classrooms into a sort of hotel room called a prophet's chamber. Staying in an empty church could be kind of spooky. Church services were on Sunday and Wednesday, so we depended on people being generous enough to allow us to stay an extra day or two until we traveled to the next church. We always had a place to sleep. On occasion, it was a camper in the church parking lot or a church member's yard.

"Are you always going to be missionaries?" one pastor asked us as we stood before the congregation. "We don't want to begin supporting missionaries who one day change their minds."

"Yes, we are always going to be missionaries," we assured him.

Many mothers of young children would object to being away from home at a time when the children needed to take their naps in their own beds. Kathy amazingly managed to care for three small children, often in other peoples' homes or while traveling by car. We brought a collapsible playpen and a nifty high chair that could be suspended precariously on the edge of any table.

Our children learned to make friends easily and played with the children of our hosts. Once or twice, we stayed on a farm. This was quite interesting for us, seeing them care for their animals. I sometimes accompanied the farmer on farm chores.

We survived those first few months on the small monthly support that came in and the offerings we received when we visited churches. Sometimes we asked the pastor if he could cash the check for us from the church offering plate so we could put gas in the car to get to the next church. We didn't have credit cards.

In the car after leaving the church, Kathy and I often discussed how much we had received. It didn't occur to us the children were listening. One day when the pastor handed me the offering check, Brian Rush spoke up in front of the pastor. "How much did we get, Papa?"

At about this time, Bob Jones University was in a Supreme Court battle regarding its policy of not allowing students to date or marry someone of a different race. The university risked losing its tax-exempt status as a religious institution, and students might no longer be able to use the G.I. bill to attend BJU. The government considered this to be a subsidy to an institution that practiced discrimination.

We stayed with a family for a few days in Colorado, and our host asked me about the Supreme Court case involving my alma mater.

"On which biblical passage is the university's prohibition against interracial dating based?"

I struggled to give an answer. Bob Jones III had appeared on the Phil Donahue show earlier that year and was asked the same thing. His response was something like, 'Where do I start? It is a principle that is all through the Bible." Frankly, I had been frustrated with Dr. Bob's response. I had never been able to see it in the Bible.

***

We were on deputation for almost two years. During this period, we visited more than two hundred churches in Kansas and adjoining states—Colorado, Missouri, Iowa—and later in the Southeast— Alabama, Florida, Mississippi, Tennessee—and on one trip up the east coast to New Jersey, Pennsylvania and Delaware. A wonderful, if taxing, experience.

It was always a surprise to see what the churches looked like. There were nice traditional-looking brick churches with steeples; others were buildings that had been re-purposed. One country church had previously been a huge chicken coop. A few churches met in rented spaces such as schools or the Elks Club. One church shared the building with a Seventh Day Adventist Church.

We sold our little house in Newton and, after a few more months of deputation in Kansas and adjoining states, moved back to Alabama.

"Any mail for us?" I asked Daddy, hoping for new financial support. We desperately needed the money for living expenses but also hoped to meet the monthly amount our mission board said we needed to live in Taiwan.

Daddy found us a house in Mobile that had not been lived in for a few years due to foreclosure. Less than a mile from my childhood home, it had been vandalized, and the pipes had frozen. Daddy contacted the owner and proposed that he repair the house if we could live in it until we departed for Taiwan. When we weren't traveling to raise funds, we lived there.

***

"Who are you, and what are you doing here?" the man asked as we sat in the donut shop across the street from the motel. The church where we had presented our ministry the night before had put us in a motel room in this small Tennessee town.

When we awakened, we saw a thick blanket of snow covering everything. We couldn't drive in this. We waited for the pastor to call and let us stay another day, but no call came. We checked out, walked to the donut shop, got some breakfast and talked about what to do next. A customer at the donut shop eyed us inquisitively. I thought his query was odd but not threatening.

"We are missionaries on deputation. We spoke in a church in the area last night. We are waiting for the snow to clear so that we can get on our way," I explained.

"I thought it might be something like that." He introduced himself as the pastor of a small church not far away. Maybe he had seen us pray before eating our breakfast. "It's going to be a while before all of this snow melts. Why don't you come to my house? My wife and children will be happy to meet you."

We got in our car and cautiously followed him through the snow to a modest home where his children played in the snow. As we talked, we found that we had a friend in common, a missionary to Germany who we had met in Kansas. We stayed there for two days, our children playing together, his wife preparing meals for us. They accepted us as if we were relatives. Finally, we said goodbye, packed up everything and headed to the next church. We never saw or heard from that family again.

When visiting churches, it was considered improper to ask directly for financial assistance, so we simply asked them to pray for us. Churches are often strapped financially, and deciding to commit to monthly financial gifts takes time, often months or years. Occasionally a pastor encouraged members to give to us individually, but many didn't like the idea because it might mean they give less to their church.

"I can't believe you did this without my permission," a pastor said to me following a service in which we had shared about our ministry. Dumbfounded, I had no idea what he was talking about. He held up a piece of paper I had placed on our display table of names and addresses of members who had requested to receive our monthly prayer letter.

"I can't have you contacting my members without my permission," he said. This related to a view that we occasionally came across. Storehouse tithing is a practice that specifies that all of a Christian's offerings go to the local church of which the person is a member. "Bring ye all the tithes into the storehouse, that there may be meat in mine house. . . ." (Malachi 3:10). I suppose he feared his congregants would donate money directly to us.

We began to develop a more pragmatic attitude. We needed financial support in order to be missionaries. One pastor was known to be an ardent Calvinist, believing God had decided everything in advance.

"When you get to Taiwan, you will discover that there are certain individuals whom God has already chosen and earmarked for Salvation," he said to us in front of his congregation. I didn't hold that view, but if the church wanted to support us, that would be fine. Apparently, God had not foreordained this particular church to support us financially.

19

The anxiety and irrational worries worsened. A troubling thought entered my mind that I had done something wrong. *Had I behaved inappropriately toward a woman whom I had encountered in a church I had visited?* Though I knew such thoughts were baseless and irrational, I had difficulty expelling them from my mind. Sometimes my mind felt like a broken record, going over and over the same awful thought.

I sought help from God for this through prayer and searching the scriptures. I tried to accept this as my thorn in the flesh and likened it to Paul's, which he asked God to remove three times, having his requests denied. "And he said unto me, my grace is sufficient for thee: for my strength is made perfect in weakness. Most gladly therefore will I rather glory in my infirmities, that the power of Christ may rest upon me." (II Corinthians 12:9)

One day, I went jogging, something I had done off and on since my bachelor days. Upon returning, my anxiety abated somewhat. I tried to run as often as I could, daily if possible, and this seemed to make it easier to dismiss the intrusive thoughts.

I was puzzled at what our mission board director said as I spoke to him by phone. "New Jersey?" I responded. That was not really in our area of the country for deputation. "I'm not sure it is advisable to drive from Alabama to New Jersey to visit one church."

"Well, they want to support a missionary in Taiwan, and I'm almost certain that if you make the trip up there, they will become regular supporters," he said. "Try to find a few other churches to visit on the way. It will be worthwhile."

We packed up the children in the fall of 1983 and headed up the east coast. We stopped by Washington, DC, a place I had never been. We visited the capitol and even went in while Congress was in session and sat in the gallery. We hadn't been there long when eleven-month-old Daniel tried to make a motion. "Mama!" We were ushered out.

We were in Fortescue, New Jersey, having dinner with a couple and the pastor from the church where we had presented our program the previous evening. The man mentioned he had been having problems which, as he described them, sounded similar to what I had been experiencing—crippling and inexplicable anxiety.

"This doctor prescribed some medicine for me, and I have been a lot better," the man said. He mentioned a particular doctor who knew how to treat the issue.

Could I be helped by medication? I always viewed my troubling thoughts as attacks from Satan, who was trying to keep me from becoming useful to God. I tucked this information away in my mind, not daring to say anything lest I disclose problems that might disqualify me from being a foreign missionary.

Fortescue, a tiny fishing village on the Delaware Bay, looked like something out of a bygone era. Aging frame houses on the edge of the bay, some on pilings that extended a few feet over the bay, stood across the road from the little church. Before leaving, Brian Rush and Margaret looked for shells along the edge of the leaning wooden seawall. They found a horseshoe crab washed up on the narrow strip of sand.

We secured the three children in their car seats and set out on the long journey back to Alabama. At Cape May, we drove onto a ferry to cross the Delaware Bay. As the ship departed the dock, we climbed the stairs to the expansive lounge area, where there were rows of seats and a snack bar. Brian Rush and Margaret scurried around, safe from the expanse of water outside. Daniel, almost a year old, played at our feet as Kathy and I took in the vastness of the Atlantic Ocean to our left and the Delaware Bay to our right.

My anxiety hung like a huge weight on my shoulders, the terrifying worries never completely absent. Satan hurled his darts to torture me, taking my mind from the task of preparing to be missionaries. I again claimed the promise of the Bible that if I resisted the devil, he would eventually flee and leave me alone.

We drove off the ferry and down the coast of Delaware, Maryland, and Virginia (the Del-Mar-Va Peninsula). We crossed the eighteen-mile-long bridge, including two tunnels, across the Chesapeake Bay into Virginia Beach. We didn't know then that we would one day live in this city.

During the hours driving back to Alabama, my thoughts returned again and again to the conversation about how medication had helped that church member. After returning to Mobile, I decided to take a chance and called the pastor of the church in Delaware and asked for his phone number.

When I reached the man, I asked the name of the doctor who had treated him. He gave me the name of a physician in Pennsylvania. He didn't ask why.

The doctor picked up the phone right away when I called. "It tends to run in families," he explained. He told me about a book, *The Masks of Melancholy* by John White, which described the many forms depression could take in an individual's life. For the first time, I felt some hope that I could be free of these dark and terrifying thoughts.

I ordered the book and began to read it at once. One example was of a man who continually feared that he had hit someone with his car and would retrace his route, again and again, to assure himself that he hadn't. This was not unlike my fears about what I might have done wrong, going over and over the situation. The book mentioned that medication could sometimes be a solution to the problem. I didn't know what kind of doctor I should see.

***

"Son, what were you doing?" an elderly woman kept saying. I stood on the side of the road, dirty and in a dazed state. I had crawled out of my car, which had rolled down an embankment and landed upside down. It all happened so fast.

"Are you alright? Who are you?" the elderly man said.

"I'm a missionary," I said.

I had been traveling alone to speak at a few churches in Tennessee and Kentucky. Daddy had allowed me to take his car so that Kathy would have a car to use while I was away for two weeks. The morning after a church service, I headed to my next engagement in Tennessee and had been driving on a stretch of a paved two-lane road. It rained lightly.

I often listened to sermon tapes while I drove, using a cassette player plugged into the cigarette lighter for power. I must have looked down to adjust the volume, and when I looked up, there was a car that had slowed right in front of me. I hit the brakes, and the car began to slide sideways. As I spun out of control, the back of the car clipped the rear end of the car in front of me, and I began to spin the other way.

I went down an embankment, and the car rolled. I landed wheels up. I scrambled out of the broken window and up the embankment. After talking to the elderly couple for a moment, I noticed the car appeared to be still running. *Was that possible, upside down?* I crawled back down the hill, reached in and turned off the key.

I sat next to the wrecker driver as we drove to the next town with the car on the flat bed of the truck. I called the pastor of the church where I had spoken the previous evening. The next morning he took me to the junkyard where the car, now totaled, had been towed so I could retrieve my belongings. I called the pastor of the church next on my schedule to visit, and he helped plan transport for me to his church in Kentucky. After the Wednesday evening service there, I flew back home to Mobile.

God, are you chastising me for something? I knew that nothing happens without God's permission, so there must be some reason for what had happened. Was God punishing me for the doubts that I sometimes had as to whether it could be true that the lost would suffer in hell forever?

Then another interpretation of the event entered my mind. I had experienced a serious accident and had come out with barely a scratch. *God, are you showing me you will protect my family and me?*

Anxious thoughts of all kinds persisted during the following weeks. I returned to what I had read in the book about medication for problems like my anxiety. I decided to mention it to our family doctor. He was especially sympathetic to clergy. In fact, he instructed his office staff not to accept a co-pay from me or my family members when we came for medical care. He accepted only the amount insurance paid.

I worried that being treated for mental health issues could come to the attention of our mission board since they handled our health plan. *How will I explain this if they ask me?* I willingly took this risk in order to get help.

"What are you reading there?" Dr. Bailey asked as he looked at my injured finger, the only noticeable outcome from the accident. I used my slight injury as a reason to visit the doctor. He must have sensed there was something else. I showed him the cover of *The Masks of Melancholy*.

"Looks like a good book," he said sympathetically. I told him about my struggles with intrusive thoughts and anxiety. He came across as knowledgeable. The seed of hope that I had felt when speaking to the other doctor by phone swelled into a tiny seedling.

He wrote me a prescription and asked me to return in a week. He also gave me the business card of a person who he wanted me to talk to—a therapist. "This person's work is to help God's helpers," he said. I put the card in my pocket, not sure what to make of this.

I sat on the edge of my bed and looked at the bottle the pharmacist had given me. What would happen when I took one of these pills? Was I going to become a different person? I had no one to ask. I told Kathy I would take one of the pills the next morning and not to expect anything from me for the day.

"I'll try one appointment and see what it is about," I told Kathy. Psychology was suspect in the religious circles in which we moved. I feared this therapist might identify something in my Christian beliefs that was the source of my problems. I had been warned again and again about the danger of liberal theology and humanism in society. *What if this person says my religion is the root of the problem? What will I do then?*

20

Bill was not a lot older than me. He dressed casually and had a beard. He looked like Jesus, warm and engaging.

"Is what we talk about private?" I asked him. He assured me that nothing I said in therapy would leave the room. "Do you think that this can be successfully treated before I leave for Taiwan in six months?" I asked Bill.

"We'll see what we can do," he said.

"The devil is attacking me and trying to prevent me from doing God's will," I said several times.

"For the time being, let's leave the devil out of this and let's see what we can do," Bill said thoughtfully. In years to come, I would often reflect on his words. I didn't know then that this would begin a different way of looking at my life and problems. Slowly I moved away from seeking a strictly religious solution and began to do what I could to understand myself and make changes to my life and outlook.

Bill had been to seminary but was much more theologically liberal than me. *I'm not going to let his liberal ideas corrupt my beliefs.* As time went by, I began to find his approach to faith and religion rather refreshing.

"The Bible is true, it has to be true!" he said one day. What he meant by true was entirely different from the literal acceptance of the frightening dogma I had been taught. I went through periods of fearing that Bill had led me astray and pronounced to him that I would not continue therapy, that I would read books and fix myself. He responded that this was fine and even recommended readings for me. But I returned. I found therapy opened up new ways of looking at life and faith, and it helped with the anxiety and depression from which I had suffered for so long.

One of the books I read was by the renowned Harvard psychologist Gordon Allport, *The Individual and His Religion*. It introduced the idea that an individual's religious outlook was determined to some degree by their personality, life circumstances and environment. This was the first time I had ever considered that my faith outlook was anything other than a discovery of an objective reality outside of me. This was enlightening—but also troubling.

The suggestion that my faith was not the universal truth threatened to pull the rug out from under everything I had based my life on. On the other hand, this helped explain why I had gravitated toward this kind of outlook in the first place and why some elements of it were so hard for me to accept.

"People must not be so bad. God became one," Bill said. He said things so different from what I heard from other religious people. I had told him people are sinful, "desperately wicked," the Bible says.

"I am unworthy of God's love," I insisted. Could I feel good about my unique abilities—Greek and music—and not feel that I had to push them to the side?

Bill recommended books on self-esteem and the pursuit of your own abilities and dreams. All of this intrigued me, but I struggled with the fear that I was venturing into dangerous waters. I started to entertain other ways of looking at myself, ways that made me feel confident in who I was. I even went to a hairstylist (instead of a barbershop) and had my hair styled.

"Decided to go punk, huh?" Diane, Kathy's sister, said when I walked into the house. Kathy had told her where I had been. I found myself able to laugh at this comment.

The cost of weekly therapy sessions concerned me. Money was tight. We had to submit a record of our expenses to our mission board each month, and I didn't want to reveal that I attended this kind of treatment. I left out that expense item. It was fifty dollars per session. My parents had given us some money each month, and I decided to use this to pay for the sessions. *My parents must have messed me up, so I will use their money to try to fix myself.* Bill told me that I could pay it whenever I was able.

***

Strangers milled around, looking at our belongings. What we wouldn't take with us to Taiwan was for sale in our driveway. We had sold a lot of stuff in Kansas when we left there more than a year ago. This was the big "going out of business" sale.

A man sorted through a box of toys I had marked fifty cents each. "Would you take twenty-five cents for this?" A mixture of anger and regret rose up in my throat. Objects always carried emotions for me, each one reminding me of the anticipation leading to its purchase, the excitement of having something new, the intrigue of learning to use it.

We purchased our tickets in November of 1984 to fly to Taiwan in January. We secured some fifty-five-gallon drums, and Daddy helped me construct round boxes that would enable us to lift them out of the drums if required for inspection when going through customs in Taiwan. There were three boxes per drum, fifteen drums in all.

We found a sturdy wooden crate, having been used to ship a boat engine, to hold things that didn't fit into barrels. "Unaccompanied Baggage, Brian McDonald, Taichung, Taiwan, REPUBLIC OF CHINA" was stenciled on each barrel and crate.

People didn't understand what we were doing and asked odd questions.

"Are you taking your car?"

"Are you taking your children?"

We didn't have the backing of a big corporation or the military to handle our logistics and security. We made our own arrangements to ship all our belongings via ocean freighter. There were a couple of missionary families in Taiwan who advised us.

During the past year, Kathy had set up a little school area in the house we lived in. There was a child's table with little chairs. There were posters on the wall above the table. She went through kindergarten curriculum with Brian Rush—who we now call BR—to prepare him for first grade. She planned to homeschool our children after we arrived in Taiwan.

The financial amount promised by churches and a few individuals inched up toward what the mission board had set as the amount we needed to live in Taiwan—$1,400.00 per month. Departure was less than two months away.

"It is going to be hard on your parents for you to go so far away," was a comment we heard a few times from family members. "There is a lot of missionary work that needs to be done right here in America." We heard these kinds of comments from people when they heard about our plans. Our parents never said anything like this, nor did they discourage us from going. We believed it was God's will that we go. The rest was in his hands.

We gathered at the small airport in Mobile on January 9, 1985. We said goodbye to our family and friends. The pastor of the small church we attended in Mobile, along with a few church members, came to the airport to see us off to Newton, Kansas. All of our family members were there. We held hands and prayed together.

I felt Mom's body tremble as she sobbed deeply when I put my arms around her. Joe put his arm around my shoulder and handed me a little card that looked as though he had been carrying it in his wallet. It had an inspirational phrase written on it.

"Maybe this will help you when you are over there," he said.

Daddy shook my hand. "Son, let me know if you need anything

at all. The last thing I want to happen is for you to be over there and not have something you need." I hugged him.

Kathy's mother and father, sisters, brother, niece and nephew were all there, and we exchanged hugs and well wishes. There was vague talk about a possible visit to Taiwan in the future.

We were in Kansas for a few days, visiting a few of the families that we were especially close to. The church gave us a big send-off. Pastor Jerry and a group of twenty or so church members drove the thirty miles from Newton to the Wichita airport to see us off.

"We Love You McDonalds," a hand-painted sign said. We managed to get the three children (now ages six, four, and two) buckled in their seats. As the plane took off, Kathy began to cry. This was the most emotion she had shown throughout the flurry of events of the last few weeks.

"What's wrong?" I asked her.

"Leaving Mobile wasn't as bad because we were going to another place, Kansas, where we knew there were people who loved us awaiting our arrival. Now we are headed to a place full of people we have never seen, who don't know us. We don't know if they will love us." The children looked on, puzzled.

I was sweating as I pulled the cart of luggage. In San Francisco, we were required to claim all of our luggage and go from the domestic to the international terminal. Kathy managed three small children while I pushed the cart, piled precariously high. Even though we had shipped so many things, we still had too much luggage and were required to pay extra.

Our plane stopped in Anchorage, and the stewardesses asked everyone to get off the plane so it could be cleaned. BR, Margaret and Daniel were asleep, and the crew kindly allowed us to stay aboard. Traveling with three small children is exhausting. We felt more and more disheveled and sweaty as the plane made its way toward Asia.

"What are those people saying?" four-year-old Margaret

asked. We began to hear other languages around us. How would these unintelligible sounds ever mean anything to us? *God, if you have called us, you will enable us to learn the language.*

Part IV
Missionary

21

We walked out of the jet-way into the cavernous airport, eyes burning from sleeplessness and craving a bath. We had to claim our baggage before going through customs. Arnie and Gary, our new colleagues, met us there when we pushed the cart piled high with luggage through the swinging doors into the arrival area.

"That's the most luggage we've ever seen anyone bring!"

I knew Gary in college at BJU but had not seen him for eight years. I had never met Arnie, though we had corresponded. We had been traveling and sleeping in our clothes for about thirty-six hours. BR, Margaret and Daniel stoically moved ahead to the next unknown destination, doing their best to smile when greeted by these new friends.

The first days in Taiwan were an adventure into a new world. Gary showed me how to activate the water heater at his house, which heated only the amount needed for a shower. Due to the time change, twelve hours, we were up and hungry in the middle of the night. I ate a bunch of roasted beans called *chan dou* and dreamt I flew through space.

Mrs. Faust (Mom Faust, as we called her) bought BR one of those padded Chinese coats with a Mandarin collar for his sixth birthday on January 18, the day after we arrived.

We stayed with Gary and his family in a village outside the city of Taichung for a week. He and his wife Mary and their four children lived above a small church he had started in a storefront. There was a big metal door that slid up into the ceiling like a garage door.

Traffic was chaotic. Buses, taxis, bicycles, motorcycles wove in and out, honking horns. We feared the two of us might not be able to manage the three children, so we purchased a two-seater stroller for Margaret and Daniel.

Gary and Mary didn't have a car, so they showed us how to use public transportation. We couldn't read the signs or speak the language, so we were careful not to venture too far. We learned to ride buses. The young woman stood at the window inside the bus sticking her head out periodically. She looked rather like a member of the female military with her uniform skirt and matching top with an envelope-style hat. She blew a whistle as the bus approached each stop.

The children took all of the changes in stride. When we were given new and odd things to eat, such as various kinds of seafood, octopus, sea cucumber or soup, Kathy and I acted like this was an amazing adventure, and they followed right along.

After a few days, we craved some familiar food. Arnie and his wife, Debbie, took us to an American steak house. It was what people in Taiwan thought Americans ate. They brought the steaks out, still cooking on a cast-iron plate, with sauce poured over the meat. Smoke rose from each plate, and we were instructed to hold our cloth napkins up to prevent the sauce from popping onto our clothes. The children thought this was a great sport. Daniel, just two years old, knelt on his chair and held up his napkin as if this were some exciting new game.

Each tiny steak, smaller than a hamburger patty, came with a fried egg and a baked potato about the size of a tangerine. This became a frequent place to eat for special occasions. We got used to the smaller portions and were aghast when we returned to the US a few years later and served baked potatoes five times the size.

All communication required interpretation. We began right away attending church services at the Lei Hu Church. We sat in the back, and one of the missionaries, usually Arnie, interpreted for us. Mom Faust sat with us. She had come to Taiwan as a woman in her sixties and had never learned the language. Since her adopted Chinese son Boya could interpret for her, she managed.

The Lei Hu Community Church had been established by Boya and Mrs. Faust ten years prior to our arrival. It had a lovely little courtyard with a fish pond. There was a parking lot, a rarity in Taiwan, for motorcycles, bicycles and a few cars.

Inside the church, oscillating electric fans hung high on the walls every six feet or so. They had strings attached so that they could be adjusted by someone standing underneath them. There were two window-style air conditioners mounted up high. During the many years we were there, they turned them on only for weddings.

The first Sunday, Kathy and I sang a song, me accompanying on guitar, as we had so many times during the preceding two years. In a way, auditioning again, but this time not to gain financial support but to be accepted into a new community. The teenagers loved BR, Margaret and Daniel, wanting to take them by the hand and walk with them or put them on their shoulders.

"That lady kept getting close to my face and saying *bu ke yi*," four-year-old Margaret said. Our three children had gone to Sunday school on one of our first Sundays. They were clueless as to what was going on and weren't attentive. I'm not sure what Margaret was doing, but the teacher repeatedly said this phrase in an intense tone. Margaret was not happy about the situation, and finally, when the teacher got close to her face again, she slapped the teacher's face— not a good start. Finally, we asked another missionary the meaning of *bu ke yi*: "Stop doing that."

I rode on the back of Gary's motorcycle as we looked for a place to live. Buses, taxis, bicycles and motorcycles swarmed around us. We found a place close to the Lei Hu Church and the language school where we would study Chinese for much of our first four-year term. Gary and Arnie alternated days stopping by our house to see if we needed anything. They helped us buy furniture, enroll in language school, etc. The plan had originally been to purchase the Faust's used car, but as we considered what all we needed, we decided we would forgo a car.

We needed a whole house full of furniture but were cautious not to spend all of our set-up fund right away. We spent a lot on an American-style refrigerator and washing machine. We bought some used furniture items from missionaries who were about to depart for furlough. The homes in Taiwan did not have built-in kitchen cabinets, so we ordered some to be made. There were no closets in any rooms, so we purchased collapsible vinyl closets that zipped up. The children slept on pallets on the floor for the first six months.

I disassembled the wooden crate and used the wood to make shelving. I used the skids from the crate to elevate the kitchen sink, which sat too low for our use. We stored the barrels on the flat roof.

"Papa, come see what we found. It's a puppet show," the children called to me from the end of the lane where we lived. Indeed, a puppet show was being performed, but no one was watching, no one except us. The puppet show faced a crude little altar with a statue of a red-faced fierce-looking warrior, and the performance was intended for whatever deity they worshipped here. There was a loudspeaker saying things we didn't understand and a person crouching and moving puppets. Even though this was near houses where people lived, no one appeared to pay attention to the performance. These altars could be seen all around Taiwan.

Also, at this dead-end was a metal drum where people would dump their food scraps. From time to time, we saw a man riding a dirty motorcycle outfitted to carry buckets which he dumped into the barrel. The barrel, filled with rice, soup and table scraps, went to a farm and fed to hogs. Occasionally we saw stray cats perched on the rim sampling the leftovers.

We gave testimonies for church services. A testimony is a person talking about what Christ means to them. Christians were few in number despite many years of missionary work in Taiwan. Less than 5 percent of the population identified themselves as Christian.

I had been through six years of formal training and had five years of experience. Over the years, I had led many in the prayer asking Jesus to come into their hearts, but the number who followed through and began regularly participating in a church were far fewer. Were we going to be able to accomplish more here than so many who have come before us?

***

Language classes started about six weeks after our arrival. My teacher showed me how to curl my tongue to make a common sound in Mandarin. This aspect of the language is hardest for non-Chinese people to master. We threw ourselves into language study, our primary job during this first term. Taiwan actually has several languages. Mandarin is used for education and in government offices as the official language of Beijing (previously known in the west as Peking or Peiping).

There are many dialects in China. The written language can be read by everyone if educated. Almost everyone in Taiwan can speak Mandarin, and it is the preferred language of youth and the college-educated. The native dialect for 80 percent of Taiwan's people is what is usually referred to as Taiwanese. In China, it is called Fukienese (pinyin: Fujianese) or sometimes Minnanese. Some of the elderly spoke Japanese since Japan previously ruled Taiwan. The indigenous people of Taiwan (often called mountain people) also had their own language. Conveniently, most could understand Mandarin, even if they didn't speak it well.

There were different views regarding which language was better for missionaries to learn and use. Mandarin definitely enabled you to communicate with the greatest number of people.

But Taiwanese was the native tongue of most of the people, and some say the language of their heart. Many elderly people felt more comfortable speaking Taiwanese.

Ni di guo yu jiang de hun hao (You speak Mandarin so well). We often heard this, even after attempting the simplest phrase. We began to attend language classes daily. I usually attended three hours per day; one hour in the morning at 7:00 a.m. and then later in the afternoon from 3:00 to 5:00. I used the time in between to study while also watching the children so Kathy could attend classes. I loved studying the language. I was determined to not only speak the language but to read and write it as well. I spent as many hours as possible drilling myself in the vocabulary, writing the characters, listening to tapes and repeating what I heard.

When speaking Mandarin, I felt somewhat liberated from the restraints I had been under starting when I was told I had to cut my hair back in high school. I felt like a different person. During my therapy with Bill, I had accepted that it was okay to take pleasure in my own abilities and uniqueness.

I sometimes forgot that I was supposed to be a missionary warning people of their eternal fate in hell if they didn't accept Jesus as savior. Was I becoming a different person than who my mission board and supporters thought I was?

We purchased a small used 50cc scooter to get around, often carrying a child or two on the back. A little school bus picked up BR and transported him to a half-day Mandarin-speaking kindergarten. He bravely went to school each day, offering no complaint; but it must have been frightening to spend the entire day with people who he couldn't understand. After a few months, I heard him using Mandarin phrases with other local children.

22

I was in a shiny new taxi in another city. I had taken the bus from Taichung and headed to the location of a speech competition for foreigners. These events took place from time to time for expatriates in the country, and I decided to give it a try.

The taxi driver scared me, driving wildly, often on the wrong side of the road, one hand honking the horn constantly. There was red betel nut juice around the driver's mouth. Chewing betel nut was common among working-class men. Sidewalks often revealed red splotches where they spit the juice.

The driver's hand, resting on the gearshift, displayed his two-inch long pinkie fingernail. I grabbed the safety handle as the car swerved again. I silently vowed to look for taxis with elderly drivers who were more cautious in the future. This guy probably had a new taxi because he wrecked the previous one.

When I started giving my speech, television cameras moved forward and practically got in my face. I guess they thought I was going to do well in the contest. Somehow, I wasn't rattled and continued as if I was used to the attention. It was quite a rush to be in the spotlight like this, if even for a moment.

"Try to look at the news this evening," I told Kathy when I called her from a payphone. "I won first place! There were TV cameras there. I might be on television." I felt proud since a number of the other contestants were students from well-known American universities, like Yale, who were in Taiwan to further their study of Mandarin. I loved who I was when I spoke this new language.

The thought that the kind and wonderful people we encountered would go to hell unless they accepted Jesus as savior tormented me. But to question this was to question the essence of the Christian faith. *I can still promote faith in Jesus Christ and for those who accept, it will be a very positive thing for them.* As with other troubling aspects of my faith, I viewed this as a mystery.

Many local people we met had never met someone from the west. Teenaged girls we encountered often combed Margaret's hair and braided it. We invited these people into our homes, even though our ability to communicate was limited. I didn't yet know the language well enough to witness to these individuals and try to convert them to Christianity. So, we were simply kind and hospitable to them.

One day we were at a park, letting BR, Margaret and Daniel play on the swings. A group of girls, probably ten years old, had just gotten out of school and were brave enough to approach our children, curious about them. When we communicated with them in our childlike Mandarin, they were thrilled. They had made friends with *foreigners*.

Kathy asked them if they wanted to come to our house and have a snack. Five of them accepted the invitation, and we walked the few blocks back to our house, where Kathy gave them cookies and juice. Their eyes were as wide as if they were at Disneyworld. One saw forks in the drawer. "Look, they really do use forks."

"Will you give us English names?" they asked excitedly. Andrea, Jennifer, Nicole, Sarah (the names of my brother's four daughters) and Angela (Kathy's niece's name). They looked on with awe as we wrote down each of their names. Most people who had studied English at all had either chosen or been given an English name, a badge of honor.

Mom Faust couldn't speak any Mandarin, so she relied on everyone having an English name so that she could remember who they were. She liked to give them biblical names. When she had exhausted the more well-known Bible names like Peter, Paul, Andrew, Mary and Martha, she used the less well-known names in the Bible: Ezekiel, Jonah, Delilah. When she named a teenaged boy Othniel, Arnie and I had to look away to hide our amusement.

The five girls stopped by from time to time, and we taught them a few words of English. As time went on, fewer and fewer of them came until, at last, only Andrea came. She continued to stop by occasionally for a couple of years and looked upon Kathy as a sort of auntie. Despite numerous invitations, she never came to church with us.

These first months in Taiwan were some of the most satisfying in my life. Every day I could see my language ability increasing. I taught English in the Bible College associated with our mission group. This consisted mostly of drilling the students in English phrases. The teaching was boring, but I enjoyed the eager students.

Arnie suggested I be a sponsor for the youth group, which met on Saturday nights at the Lei Hu Church. At first, I understood maybe 10 percent of what they said, so being some kind of advisor to them was rather ludicrous. But I improved rapidly. Later, one young man said he didn't remember when I couldn't speak Mandarin.

I sweated profusely as I sawed through the burglar bars to install the tiny air conditioner in our smallest room so we could all sleep there. It was May, and we were learning to live in a tropical climate. The house had neither heat nor air conditioning. We didn't think an air conditioner was essential when we budgeted our money, but it was. I purchased it from a departing missionary for twenty-five dollars. All five of us slept in that room the first summer.

We had been in Taiwan for seven months, and it was getting close to the time for BR to start first grade. Our original plan was for Kathy to home-school the children. We had tried this for the kindergarten curriculum during deputation and found that it was quite stressful for a mother of three to do while maintaining the rigors of deputation travel and continuing to care for a family. In addition, she attended language school daily.

Some other missionaries sent their children to a school run by one of the missionaries. This was a sort of a one-room schoolhouse program in which students worked at their own pace in little study carrels. Grades 1-12 in the same room with an attendant who walked around and answered questions. But there was another option for BR, or was there?

We could walk to Morrison Academy from our house if we wound our way through the rice paddies. This school was founded for missionary children in 1952. It had a beautiful campus with grades K-12. It offered a full curriculum, including band, chorus, art and sports. The teachers, mostly Americans, were all qualified teachers who came for the express purpose of teaching missionary children.

So why would we have ever considered anything other than this wonderful school right in our backyard? One reason was the fundamentalist missionaries considered the school to be liberal and recommended against sending our children there. Gary and Arnie said that our mission board would not approve.

The other problem was that Morrison Academy was expensive to those who were not one of the missionary groups that ran the school. The monthly support we had been advised to raise didn't include any amount for tuition. We were encouraged to teach them ourselves.

"I really want to send BR to Morrison Academy," Kathy insisted. I felt the same way. This was our first child to go to school, and we wanted him to have the best experience that we could reasonably give him. As far as the cost, we would trust God to provide. We didn't tell the mission board.

I preached my first sermon using Mandarin after we had been in Taiwan for almost a year. It had literally taken me the entire time I had studied Mandarin to prepare for this one sermon. I preached for about twenty minutes. It was an exhilarating experience. My text was Psalms 37:23–24. "The steps of a good man are ordered by the Lord: and he delighteth in his way. Though he fall, he shall not be utterly cast down, for the Lord upholdeth him with his hand."

Kathy's parents wanted so much to come to Taiwan to visit us, especially her father. He had suffered several small strokes and had become quite frail, had difficulty walking, talking and had lost some use of one arm. Kathy's mother could not dissuade him from making the trip.

The taxi driver looked at the card and looked at me as if confused. He adjusted his glasses and looked at it again. I had helped my elderly father-in-law into the front seat of the taxi with great effort. The taxis in Taiwan were small, and I had to push his head down to wedge him in. Kathy, her mother, Margaret and Daniel were in the back seat. "Yes, that is the address we want to go to," I assured the driver. He expelled air in a somewhat exasperated manner. Then, as BR and I watched, he pulled the taxi forward for one hundred feet or so, made a U-turn at the light and let his fare disembark on the other side of the highway. BR and I took the crosswalk and met them on the other side.

The restaurant that we wanted to get to was indeed across the street, but to get to it involved using an elevated crosswalk, and Mr. Harris was unable to climb the stairs. I wasn't going to try to walk him across eight lanes of traffic in some of the worst traffic in the world.

Kathy's mother worried that in the event he passed away while in Taiwan, it could be a nightmare bringing his body back. I promised to look into it, which I did. But such things are difficult to get a firm answer on. The more I inquired, the more convoluted the answer became. I couldn't really get an answer.

"If such a thing were to happen, there should be no problem at all," I told my mother-in-law. Their visit during Christmas of 1985 was wonderful. The children remember their Granddaddy throwing his shoes down the stairs because he couldn't put them on himself.

Prior to losing some of his ability to speak, Kathy's father never withheld his opinion on anything. Now, when he rode with me in the car in Taiwan traffic, which could be described in no less terms than total chaos, he tried to react to the crazy drivers but couldn't summon the words in time before another motorcycle, car or taxi darted in front of us.

He was often thirsty due to one of his many medications. When we were sightseeing in some little village, I asked a shopkeeper for a drink of water for him. The shopkeeper courteously brought him a small glass of boiling water.

"That water wouldn't even put out a fire!" Mr. Harris, a retired fireman, said. When we took them on a trip by train, it was challenging getting him on and off the trains, which didn't stop for long.

Upon returning to the US, his health steadily deteriorated, and by January of 1987, Kathy made a trip back to the US to see him. She took Daniel with her, and I stayed behind with BR and Margaret. Daniel kept asking for a *ping guo*, something he often ate since attending the local pre-school. Kathy's mother learned to recognize this word and gave him an *apple* whenever he said this.

Two months later, in April, Kathy's father passed away. Kathy made a brief trip back for the funeral. Some of the Chinese Christians in Taiwan and other missionaries donated to help with the cost of these trips. Most of these people had little money to spare. This was a function of their faith and devotion. They believed that we were God's servants among them.

23

Our home had three floors. The first floor was the kitchen and living room. On the second floor were two rooms and on the third floor were two more rooms. A stairway led up to a flat roof covered by a fiberglass awning. I built shelves in the stairwell for us to store things we didn't use regularly. Anything left on the roof was covered in thick dust after a few weeks.

I made one of the third-floor rooms into a study, and the other was a bedroom for BR and Daniel. Margaret's bedroom was on the second floor, along with one for Kathy and me. Each room had a sliding door to a balcony. On the back of the house, the balconies had burglar bars. There was a place to put a padlock on the bars, but I didn't do that. I didn't like the idea of being locked in if there were a fire.

It was around 11:30 on a Sunday night. The kids were all asleep, and Kathy and I were in bed. We had been in Taiwan maybe a year and a half at this point. The telephone rang. We had not had a telephone for the first year, and now having one was a great convenience.

"Who could that be?" Kathy asked. I reached for the phone.

"Pastor Brian, we are here at the Sunday morning worship service, and this call is being broadcast to the congregation." It was Pastor Jerry in Kansas. *Yikes, how could I have forgotten this?* The church in Kansas was having their annual missionary emphasis and

Pastor Jerry had written and asked if he could call us at this time and broadcast our call for the congregation during a service.

At that very moment, as fate would have it, I was right in the middle of knowing my wife in the biblical sense. I was mortified. They couldn't see us, but I felt that I had been caught with my pants down. I could barely summon words to speak. Kathy covered her face with her hands and suppressed laughter.

"What time is it over there, Pastor Brian?" Pastor Jerry asked.

"Near the midnight hour." I imagined the eager faces of the congregants, listening with anticipation to the voice of their beloved missionary. I pulled on my pajamas and sat down on the bed and tried to get hold of myself. *They don't know what I was doing. Anyway, I wasn't doing anything wrong.* Kathy looked at me as if she were waiting for a comedian to tell the next joke.

"Kathy's here, let me have her say hello to everyone." I handed Kathy the phone and tried to compose myself. After saying a few words of greeting, Kathy returned the receiver to me.

"Let's hear you recite John 3:16 in Chinese." Pastor Jerry spoke his request into my ear. I don't remember him mentioning that I should be prepared for this. I had read it in Chinese but hadn't memorized it. *Oh well, no one there understands Mandarin, at least I don't think so.* I remembered the first few words of the verse since it was part of a song we had learned. I said these words and then mumbled some other words. We continued the conversation for a few more minutes.

"Okay, Pastor Brian, I guess we are going to sign off now," said Pastor Jerry. He ended the call, and I fell onto the bed, exhausted. We laughed and laughed.

I wanted to surprise the children by putting a ping pong table on the roof. I installed plastic chicken wire all around so that errant balls did not need to be retrieved from three floors down. I did this while they were at school. There was almost never a reason to go up on the roof, so they didn't expect anything.

The ping-pong table proved a big hit with our children and others who came over. We got pretty good at the game, a popular activity in Asia. We did everything we could to make life as fun as possible for our children. We didn't want them to miss anything just because they were missionary kids.

"Papa, I want a ramp to practice skateboarding on." The skateboard craze that seemingly every boy goes through somehow found BR and his classmates in Taiwan. I built a ramp where he could learn to do tricks.

"Cool," he said. It wasn't long before he was on to the next fad.

Kathy shopped at the open market a few blocks from our house. Vegetables, poultry, seafood of every kind, and fish still alive. Going to the market never ceased to be an adventure. You could see all kinds of sea creatures swimming in buckets. Poultry cackled in cages under a plank where the vender cut up another bird. A washing machine-looking contraption had rubber fingers protruding all around. A slain and scalded chicken would be thrown into the machine, which rotated back and forth, rubbing the feathers off.

Kathy visited the market in the mornings because nearly all of the vendors closed up and left by noon. Traditionally, local housewives went to the market and bought what was needed for that day. Kathy tried to buy a week's worth and put it in the refrigerator and freezer. Freezing food was not common in Taiwan, and the vendors were amazed at all of the meat she bought. "You must be having a huge crowd for dinner."

Kathy did her best to introduce us to local things she had seen or heard about. Chinese ate tiny dried fish that still had the heads on them. Our children had eaten a lot of unusual things attending the local kindergarten. I was reluctant to put the head of the fish in my mouth.

Daniel was used to it. "Go ahead Papa, eat the face."

We learned from the other missionaries where we could buy items that Americans preferred: some condiments, shakable salt, western-style cookies, etc. Milk was expensive, and we eventually learned to drink powdered milk with our cereal, something we could only get when we took a trip to the capital city Taipei.

Mien bao, mien bao (bread, bread). Each afternoon, we heard a woman's voice on a loudspeaker. She pushed a cart with various kinds of bread, both sweet and savory. She had a baby tied to her back. Since she pushed the cart and made slow progress, there was time for BR, Margaret and Daniel to ask for some money and go out and buy a sweet bun.

One day, Margaret asked if she could go to the home of a neighborhood friend and play.

"Sure," I said. "Do you know our phone number in case you need to call me?" She confidently recited the number in Mandarin. "Can you say it in English?" I asked. I could see the wheels turning in her head as she slowly said the numbers in English. "Be home by 5:30," I reminded her. She turned to scamper out the door, then hesitated. "How do I say that in Mandarin?"

The mother of Margaret's little friend asked if it was all right if she took Mai Jia Li (Margaret's Chinese name) to a movie with her little girl. Kathy and I glanced at each other. Should we allow this? Movie theaters were forbidden in our circles, though with the advent of VCR players, many watched the same movies at home.

"Oh, thank you for the invitation. That is so kind of you. But, we can't allow Mai Jia Li to attend a movie theater," I explained. I saw the perplexed look on the woman's face. I'm sure she wondered what could possibly be wrong with attending a Disney movie.

"Oh, I understand," she said politely, though I'm sure she didn't.

I headed out for my run one morning before it got too hot. As I trotted along, I came upon a woman straining under the weight of a pole across her shoulders with a bucket of vegetables hanging from each end. She headed to the market to sell her garden produce. Further down the road, I passed some new construction, ever present in Taiwan. Men stood on bamboo scaffolding and reached down for buckets of cement being mixed by women at ground level. The men grinned at me, revealing teeth red from chewing betel nut. Their skin was deep brown from their hours working in the tropical sun. The women had every inch of their skin covered in cloth to avoid their skin becoming dark. I couldn't recognize they were women except that I knew women laborers covered themselves in this manner.

As I jogged past the residential area and toward the nearby rice paddies, I found myself running by a small village that reminded me of pictures of China long ago. A woman bent over a ribbed stone scrubbing clothes, and children called out to me, "*Mei guo ren, mei guo ren*" (American, American). A teenage girl squatted by the roadside gutter, pouring a pot of water over her head as she washed her long blue-black hair.

I went down a narrow pathway with mud-filled rice paddies on either side. Men and women, wearing cone-shaped bamboo hats, stooped over and pushed tiny rice seedlings into the oozing mud. One worker walked behind a machine that did the same task, only more efficiently.

Ahead I saw a traditional U-shaped farm home. Homes of this design date back to the Ching Dynasty, China's last period of having an emperor. Through the open door of the house, I saw an altar from which incense burned in worship of ancestors or a god that protects farmers.

I passed through a village where people sat in front of their homes doing some kind of piece work that would go back to a factory to be completed—gadgets, clothing, toys. One elderly lady squatted, putting eyelets in sneakers. I moved to the side of the road to make room for a woman pushing a cart full of blue jeans. I encountered a group of students headed to school, all wearing identical uniforms, including yellow hats.

"Hullo, hah ah you?" one ventured, and they giggled excitedly when I responded in kind. I took a different route back home on a busy roadway. Cars, trucks, buses and scores of motorcycles whizzed by. As I neared the lane where our home was, I passed a shop where little houses made of bamboo and paper were being assembled. These dollhouse-looking structures would be burned in a ritual of ancestor worship.

I approached our house with its red gate. Nearly all the gates were red, being an auspicious color for Chinese people. Some still displayed the paper banners above and on each side, left over from Chinese New Year. Our gate led to a short walk to our front door. There was also a gate that could be opened for a car, though it would be a tight fit. Our dog, *Shao Hei* (Little Blackie), stood inside the gate, wagging her tail, excitedly welcoming me home.

***

My parents came and spent a month with us at Christmas time in 1986. We had been in Taiwan for almost two years, and we drove them around the island, visiting various sites. We had purchased a small van, largely with the help of funds from my parents. Mom's anxiety made traveling in Taiwan extremely taxing for her and stressful for us. She clutched the handle in the car, and red-faced, she exhibited a look of pure terror.

We decided to take them to the city of Kaohsiung in the southern part of Taiwan, a two-hour drive by car. As we neared our destination, we encountered one of the worst traffic jams I have ever experienced. Apparently, a tunnel had flooded, and traffic tried to find alternative routes. Motorcycles poured out of a little alley, hundreds and hundreds of them, all headed straight for us.

"It looks like ants coming out of an ant bed," Daddy said. Cars went in opposite directions in the same lane with bicycles, motorcycles. Pedestrians moved in every direction between them. "Lord have mercy," Daddy said over and over. Daddy and the rest of us thought it was quite something to witness. Mom thought otherwise. When we finally got to our hotel, we discussed going back out that evening for dinner.

"I'm not going anywhere. You guys can go, I'll stay here." Mom was emphatic.

As it turned out, it was fortuitous that Mom and Daddy didn't go that night. We had some Chinese friends who lived in the area and wanted to meet up with us. They took us to a night market. An entire street temporarily turned into a bazaar with vendors selling everything imaginable, clothes, toys, books, electronics, food and almost anything else. Traditional herbal medicines were displayed, as were live snakes. There was a chimpanzee who smoked a cigarette.

Our friends had a little girl the same age as Margaret, who by now spoke Mandarin quite well, having attended the local kindergarten. The two little girls walked along, holding hands chatting non-stop. I had Daniel by the hand, and BR walked ahead, exploring.

I looked around to call Margaret and her little friend to catch up, and I didn't see them. I retraced our steps and still couldn't find them. I shouted. "Margaret, *Mai jia li.*" Nothing. Kathy and I looked at each other with alarm. It is impossible to explain the sea of people we saw in every direction. We decided that we should split up and look for them.

"Have you seen a little Chinese girl and a little foreign girl holding hands and walking along here?" I asked every vendor. Most shrugged. *What if they had been abducted?* I tried not to think what that could mean. We went down every side street. Nothing. We had been searching for forty-five minutes or so when I heard our friend call our names.

"I found them," she shouted as she ran toward us. She had used a pay phone and called home, and her elderly mother said the girls were there. Someone had taken them to a police station. Her little girl knew her home phone number and called home. Relieved, though shaken, we headed back to the hotel. We never told my parents what had transpired that night.

There were lighter times during my parents' visit. We visited a place where you could dress in the clothes of ancient China and have your picture taken. Mom and Daddy dressed up as a Chinese Emperor and Empress. The young photographer was horrified when, lifting the head-dress off my mother's head, her wig came off with it. Mom and the rest of us howled with laughter.

24

I had stopped taking the medication for anxiety and depression after we had been in Taiwan for a year or so. I was doing great and didn't feel I needed it. But, at around the two-year mark, some fears and anxieties slowly returned. Perhaps the reality that the thrill of language study wouldn't last forever began to dawn on me. I was going to have to do missionary work at some point, converting the lost. I began to see a pattern with my anxiety. When I faced uncertainty of some kind, my anxiety manifested itself with irrational worries.

What if I do something terribly wrong that would disqualify me from being a missionary. But I have no desire to do something like that. What if I did something inappropriate with one of the female students? Had I done or desired to do so? No, then why does this thought enter my mind? As in the past, I reviewed each encounter and reassured myself that nothing had happened, only to have to do this again when the thought returned.

I had continued to send Bill, my old therapist, a few dollars each month to pay off what I owed for the therapy prior to coming to Taiwan. I didn't mind; it had been well worth it. I wrote to Bill and told him that some of the symptoms had returned and asked if he had any suggestions. After exchanging a few letters, we decided to talk on the phone at an appointed time. Taking into account the twelve-hour time difference, we indeed had a conversation of over

an hour. I felt encouraged that I could get back to where I had been
two years earlier.

At the end of our talk, I agreed to write Bill a letter and tell him
how I was doing and how I had applied some of the strategies we
had discussed. I began composing a letter, writing some each day. I
wanted to wait and mail it when I could tell Bill it was working, that
I was getting better.

"Do you know someone named Bill?" my mother asked, giving
his last name as we talked on the phone. I had never told my parents
I had been in therapy, so I was a bit taken aback.

"Yes," I said tentatively.

"He died in an accident on Saturday," she said.

I got off the phone as quickly as possible and attempted to take
this in. The things I discussed with Bill were extremely personal and
private. Things I would have been ashamed to tell anyone else. I had
questioned the assumptions that had been the foundation of my life
to that point. I had come to view Bill as my guide, a companion on
my life journey.

Bill had gone fishing with a friend. As he walked along the
roadway back to his car, he was struck by a passing car and killed.
As the news of Bill's death sunk in, my thoughts went to the
conversation we had a few months earlier. He made the effort to call
me from the other side of the world and never mentioned a charge
for the international call. But he had never heard back from me.
Now it was too late.

His request that I write a letter was for my benefit. I knew that.
Kathy was the only one with whom I could share my devastation.

"You'll always have the things you learned from Bill." Kathy
tried to console me. I corresponded with Bill's wife, expressing
my condolences. I requested she send me a photograph of him. I
took it to a local artist who had previously done charcoal drawings
of our children. The result was an amazing likeness, his curly
beard, kind eyes and understanding smile. But I never displayed

the picture; it just didn't seem appropriate. I needed to move ahead on my own two feet.

***

I discussed my role in the mission work with my colleagues now that language study was coming to an end. We had planned to study the language for two years and then move to the city of Kaohsiung, several hours south, to establish a new church. Kaohsiung, a seaport, was known for the dismantling and scraping of decommissioned ships from all over the world.

Boya and Mom Faust returned from a yearlong furlough and were surprised at how quickly we had learned the language. They offered to take us on a trip to Kaohsiung to survey the area for a new church. After making the trip, we made preliminary plans for the move. I began to feel uneasy. *Were we ready to launch out on our own in an unfamiliar city?* I had preached only a handful of sermons in Mandarin to date, and all with the help of my teachers. I discussed with the other missionaries my need for more experience ministering in Chinese before setting out on my own. They were understanding and agreed to my teaching for the next two years at the Bible College, then moving forward to establish a new church after our first furlough.

A big part of my hesitation about striking out on our own was that I did not want to face the responsibility of persuading people to believe in Christianity. In my role at Lei Hu Church and the Bible College, I worked with people who already professed to be Christians. I no longer believed that people who did not embrace Christianity would be damned to hell. *What kind of missionary doesn't even believe the basic message that is supposedly the reason for being a missionary in the first place?*

Kathy's sister Diane helped find books that I requested and mailed them to me. One such book was by M. Scott Peck, *The Road Less Traveled.* Though Peck's writing is not overtly religious, he emphasizes the concept of grace. He suggested that one's life is directed by a loving and compassionate concept—grace. Peck's emphasis on grace comforted me.

The orthodox Christianity in which I had been schooled also recognized grace, usually defining it as unmerited favor—i.e., it cannot be earned. But the punitive nature of God was also taught as a counterbalance to grace. If someone's behavior did not measure up to what was expected of a person who had been a recipient of grace, then whether this person had truly been regenerated—born again— was in doubt. Faith that did not produce appropriate behavior was not genuine faith.

Another book by Peck, *A Different Drum*, posited stages through which a person of faith or belief will likely pass. I could no longer conjure up an unwavering belief in the basic teachings of the Christian faith as I had previously. From Peck's analysis, what I had experienced was a natural, even healthy step in the development of one's faith outlook. This I found comforting and reassuring.

At my ordination, Pastor Jerry said that "if this candidate ever ceases to believe the doctrines that he is affirming today, he should return his ordination to this church." Now, as I thought of these words, they sounded absurd to me. *Could a person continue to think exactly the same throughout life?* I felt guilty that I was not the person many people thought I was.

While my religion might consider me an apostate—someone who has denied the faith—I might actually be healthier than the rigidly religious person who resists following reason out of fear of denying the faith. Peck cited James Fowler's book *Faith Development* as the source of this approach to faith.

Fowler posits that an individual will find their outlook changing and evolving throughout life, moving away from concrete concepts received from others and toward an outlook that takes into account one's own life experiences. When I considered my religious journey, this made sense.

During my time in Taiwan, I realized the Christian faith could be expressed in different ways. I encountered beliefs and views that were considerably different from my own. My outlook was expanding, but I had pledged myself to a set of Christian beliefs. My financial support came from churches and individuals who believed I was in Taiwan to propagate these beliefs and convert others to Christianity. I agonized over how to reconcile what I now believed—or did not believe—in my heart and mind with what was expected of me as a missionary.

My thoughts alternated between thinking I could no longer sincerely articulate the traditional Christian missionary message on the one hand and, on the other hand, being unwilling to deny that believing in Christ had altered my life in a positive way as a teenager. Deciding to follow Christ had changed me, and this was the message I came to Taiwan to share.

I had always dreamed that my family and I could sing and perform music together, like the family we used to visit in South Carolina. So we entered a contest in which expatriates performed traditional Chinese songs. The local people loved to see foreigners dressed in traditional Chinese clothes, imitating Chinese culture. Our Family Von McDonald was well received, and we actually appeared on television. For a while, strangers on the street often called to us, "I saw you on television!"

Kathy and I spent many hours making an audio cassette of some of our duets. We recorded in a studio made for spoken broadcasts, with me playing the guitar simultaneously. Our tape had ten songs, some English and some Chinese. It was titled *Living for Jesus*. We gave them as gifts or sold them during our furlough when visiting the churches that supported us.

My language skills progressed, and I preached and taught regularly. I avoided subjects that emphasized that only those who believed would be accepted into heaven. Instead, I preached about how to be joyful, how to get along with others, how to have a happy family, etc.

There was the occasional language *faux pas*. Once I spoke from the passage that said husbands are to give honor to the wife as unto the weaker vessel . . . (I Peter 3:7). I explained that the word weaker in this context actually referred to something delicate, something to be valued and protected, not inferior. I used the illustration of a beautiful flower vase that one might put on a high shelf lest it be damaged. After the service, one of the men pulled me aside.

"Pastor Mai, Chinese women detest being called a flower vase. This indicates a woman who is beautiful to look at but of no other use."

I may have been one of the few conservative evangelical preachers who said doubting your faith or doubting God did not mean you were not saved but could, in fact, be healthy. I emphasized that we persevere in spite of our doubts and fears. This resonated with many people while causing raised eyebrows in others. People don't expect the preacher to condone doubt.

Another way I avoided troublesome topics was to become an entertaining speaker. I told many stories, often humorous. Humor is tricky when speaking a second language. Not all stories were intended to be funny. I took the philosophy that a story could be used to convey a message without expressly stating that point. People can find themselves inside a story and draw their own conclusions or lessons.

My sermons had little of the Bible-quoting that characterized most evangelical preaching. Because of this, my messages were more palatable to people, making me a popular speaker. This was met with some consternation by the more orthodox members who viewed themselves as well-versed in their religion and wanted to hear the tenets of the faith proclaimed.

"What is the point of giving inspiring messages to people if they are going to hell because they are not warned what awaits those who do not accept Jesus as Savior?" one church leader said to me one day. This was the conundrum I faced.

Three different families from the church in Kansas visited us in Taiwan during our first term. We couldn't believe they had come all the way to Taiwan to see us. Of course, it was an adventure for them. But I could not get away from the fact that they supported us because we were there to proclaim the beliefs that they held dear.

"They love us because of who we are, not what we believe," Kathy assured me. There was truth in this, but I knew our relationship would be forever changed if I were to deny or even question this belief system. I believed they loved and admired me so much because I did what their faith enjoined upon all believers, taking the gospel to every person in the world. I secretly felt unworthy of this love.

One of the ironies of being a member of such a faith community is that there is indeed a great deal of love and support. But it is contingent upon your professed allegiance to a set of beliefs. If you deny those beliefs, you are at best pitied and possibly shunned.

***

The ship rolled and pitched as we crossed the rough waters between Taiwan and China. We were on our way to the Pescadores, a sparsely inhabited group of islands that belong to Taiwan.

"Rub some of this on your temples." The lady said as she took a small bottle of "Green Oil" from her purse. Green Oil has a pungent mint smell, and the people of Taiwan use it much like we use aspirin, a remedy for many ailments. Eager for relief from nausea, Kathy took her advice and passed the bottle to me and each of the children who did likewise. We endured the trip and arrived smelling very minty.

The Pescadores, or Penghu as it is called in Chinese, is a small cluster of islands in the straits between Taiwan and China. The air was fresh and free from pollution, and there were relatively few people. We rented motor scooters and rode around the main island (two children on a scooter with me and one with Kathy).

Farmers had spread their rice out on the road to dry. There were almost no cars, and the occasional motor scooter had no problem going around on the shoulder. We had dinner with some local people who were curious to meet foreigners who could speak Chinese.

"Oh, don't do that," they said when I started to turn over the fish to get to the meat on the other side. They explained that in a fishing culture, it might bring bad luck because turning the fish was akin to a boat turning over in the ocean.

People who live by the ocean and make their living from the sea live a life that can be dangerous. They are often quite superstitious. We heard the sound of firecrackers coming from a fishing boat leaving the harbor and were told this was to scare away evil spirits.

When we told them we were missionaries, they accepted this as a matter of fact. To have begun to evangelize them would have felt disrespectful to me. The religion in Penghu was a mixture of Buddhism and other traditional beliefs of the local area. We visited a temple that housed a huge pond full of sea turtles, animals revered because of their long lives.

We celebrated Thanksgiving that year at Morrison Academy with a potluck dinner for all the American missionaries. We sang a few hymns and American songs. It was fun and relaxing to speak only English. We had resisted the temptation to hang out with other Americans too much during our first term. We were in Taiwan to minister to the local people and didn't want to appear to congregate only with other foreigners.

"Papa, can I ask you a question?" Daniel looked up at me. I was saying bedtime prayers with Daniel, now five years old. We tried to have family devotional time most days and said bedtime prayers with the children. As parents, we wanted to be alert to these impromptu moments when we could discuss spiritual matters with our children.

"Sure, Daniel, what do you want to ask?" I said.

"Superman wears his underpants on the outside, right?" he said.

I scratched my head as if contemplating the matter. "I never really thought about it, but you're right, he does." I said.

The monthly memos we received from our mission board cautioned against working together with other groups that were either liberal or compromising with liberals. More and more, I found it absurd to think that associating with the other missionaries we met could somehow compromise our faith.

The road across the dense mountains to the other side of the island of Taiwan was known to be quite treacherous. From time to time, buses, trying to make good time, failed to successfully negotiate a turn and toppled down the mountain. Frequent landslides covered part of the road, preventing passage for a period of time, so a motorcycle was the recommended mode of travel.

Dan, a fellow missionary, and I decided to make a trip on our motorcycles, to ride across the winding road to Hehuan Mountain, one of the highest peaks in Taiwan. We hastily decided the time was right to ride up the mountain from the northwest and down the other side before returning to Taichung from the south, a two-day trip.

"Why don't you take BR with you? It would be a wonderful experience for him," Kathy said as I readied my things for the trip. I appreciated Kathy's attitude, always wanting the children to have every experience possible, unlike my mother, whose instinct was to veto any idea that was conceivably dangerous. After growing up with a mother who wouldn't even let me take swimming lessons because I might drown, I loved it that Kathy was so gung-ho about adventurous activities for the children.

"Take him along," she said. "I'll pack him a few things in his backpack."

"Why not?" I said.

The further we rode away from the city of Taichung, the more the road began to snake through the increasingly mountainous terrain. As we reached higher elevation, we rounded sharp turns, often revealing fruit orchards in terraced fields beside the two-lane highway. We rode all day, the weather getting cooler as we reached higher elevation.

We were craving some rest when we found a little hostel not far from the ascent to Hehuan Mountain. After a good night's sleep, we planned to set out in the morning to make the climb. There was no heat in Taiwan buildings, and our room was chilly. We slept with all of our clothes and winter coats on.

The next morning we cranked our motorcycles and started up the mountain. Taiwan doesn't allow motorcycles larger than 150cc, and my Kwang Yang cycle was 125cc. Dan's did okay, but with the added weight of BR on the back, my motorcycle struggled.

"How much further is it?" nine-year-old BR moaned in my ear. The excitement of the ride had passed, and he had grown weary of hanging on to me.

"I don't really know," I said. "Not too much further, I hope." With the motorcycle in its lowest gear, we slowed to a crawl, the motor laboring, sounding as if it might quit. I steered back and forth like a switchback train rather than trying to go straight up the steep incline. BR and I got off and walked beside the cycle up the steepest portions.

We finally reached the top. Dan pointed to a building that looked as though it might be a lodge of some kind. "Let's see if we can get something to eat." Inside, the food consisted of a hot water dispenser and some dried noodles.

"Okay, let's head down the mountain," Dan said. We agreed, it was chilly on the mountain, and we looked forward to getting back to warmer air. I felt BR's weight against my back as I used the gears to slow the bike lest the brakes overheat as gravity pulled us down the mountain.

"I think this is the best beef noodle soup I've ever had," BR said as we sat in the little roadside café in the first village we came to at the bottom of the mountain. We still had a long ride ahead before we got home. We arrived late on the second day, exhausted but satisfied with the experience.

The end of our first term approached, and I didn't relish returning to the US for furlough. The person I was when I arrived in Taiwan more than three years ago and the person I had become were two entirely different people. I didn't want to return to being the former.

25

We returned to the US in June of 1988 for furlough.

"Would you please sign my Bible?" A little boy looked up at me expectantly following a service in which I had talked about being a missionary. I knew people sometimes asked preachers and missionaries to autograph their Bibles. Did I deserve to be revered in this way?

The purpose of this furlough was ostensibly to have a break from the work of being a missionary and to report to the churches that financially supported us. In reality, we also needed to secure more financial support. We had been in Taiwan for three years and five months. It was going to be a whirlwind of visiting churches that already supported us and also visiting new ones.

"Brothers and sisters, these are God's servants who have obeyed the great commission to take the Gospel to the ends of the earth." We were often introduced in this manner, being received like returning heroes by the churches who had supported us.

"God will bless any church which supports missionaries," a pastor said. Some churches had a Missionary Pantry—a room stocked with all kinds of items a family might need: toiletries, clothing, kitchen items, even toys. We were allowed to shop free of charge.

Our first furlough stop was in Kansas. Pastor Jerry urged the church to help us. The church provided us with a car to use during our stay in the US.

Being treated so royally felt wonderful. But I felt like an imposter. I no longer embraced the belief that those who did not believe in Christ were destined for hell. I struggled with depression and anxiety, had taken medication, and attended therapy, certainly not consistent with an image of the missionary hero. Being a sincere and open person is important to me. But it wouldn't work to be honest about my changing faith.

During our furlough year (extended from the original plan of six months), we visited dozens and dozens of churches. This time, Kathy and the children could not always accompany me since the children were in school. Without my family singing together, I was just another missionary talking about mission work in a foreign country, which was probably boring. In addition, this required me to talk more about evangelizing the lost.

We were based in Mobile, and Kathy and I lived in the small two-room cottage in my parents' backyard, Granny's cottage. The children stayed in my parents' home across the yard. It was a challenging arrangement, especially on school days.

When you move back home as an adult with your children in tow, there is likely to be friction. My mom sometimes acted hurt if we weren't there for dinner or if we spent time at Kathy's mother's house. Joe and his family (he had six children) lived in the same neighborhood, and my parents had taken a very active role in their lives. They were perhaps more accustomed to my parents' ways of doing things. I thought Mom was sometimes less patient with BR, Margaret and Daniel.

I continued to experience depression and anxiety. I returned to counseling with a colleague of Bill's. I guess your first therapist is like a first love. Other therapists fall short by comparison. But my new therapist pushed me to venture beyond my prior concept of God. I continued to expand my beliefs. People who saw me speak and sing in churches and at banquets saw only a self-assured missionary. Something quite different was going on inside of me.

When I asked whether there were questions from the audience, I often heard the same ones. I learned to tilt my head as if in deep thought and wrinkle my brow, carefully considering what was asked, then respond with a thoughtful answer. To this day, speaking in front of a group of people, no matter how large, is not something I fear.

Our three children attended a private religious school, the one my brother's six children attended. This made for an easier transition into the US school setting. As missionary children, our kids were treated as quasi-celebrities. They had lived in a faraway place, learned to speak a foreign language and had eaten exotic things. BR, Margaret and Daniel seemed to take the heightened attention in stride.

Am I wasting my life with the identity of Christian minister and missionary? I faced an existential dilemma. I loved speaking Chinese and living in Taiwan but hated being a spokesman for Christianity, especially the fundamentalist variety. Had I not chosen this path, I wouldn't have gone to Taiwan.

I desperately sought some way to feel more comfortable with what I was doing with my life. But it wasn't only about me. Kathy was also a missionary and felt a calling to be in Taiwan. She really loved the people and our lives there.

If I abandoned Taiwan and left the ministry, what would I do for a career? I searched for some way to transition to something else. I loved music and played trombone well, but I had no formal training that would qualify me to be a music teacher.

I explored how I might somehow go back to school and study psychology or counseling. I had benefitted from therapy and read many self-help and psychology books. Trying to understand myself through the knowledge of experts was so refreshing after years of relying completely upon the Bible, religious teachers and religious materials.

I learned of a program from Liberty University through which one could earn a master's degree in counseling. While still very conservative, Liberty had become a landing place for some people for whom Bob

Jones University had become too rigid. Liberty had developed a forward-looking program whereby a degree could be earned mostly by distance learning, something quite innovative at the time.

My alma mater, BJU, was not accredited. The explanation always given for this was that to seek accreditation would require them to compromise their beliefs. Consequently, some universities did not accept a BJU graduate for further study. But Liberty was accredited and would accept my degree. I saw this as my best chance to start studying something that might set me on a different path.

I took two courses while finishing out the furlough, both completed by viewing lectures on videotapes. Preparing to do something a little different with my life in the future gave me hope. I envisioned myself continuing in some kind of Christian ministry, only one in which I would be a counselor, not a preacher.

Through the program, I studied approaches to counseling that purported to be consistent with a Christian worldview. I also studied theories of psychology, personality development and mental illness from established secular theorists, including Freud, Adler, Erickson, Maslow, Kohlberg, and others.

We paid for the classes out of our monthly missionary financial support, a substantial sum. Kathy encouraged me as I searched for a way to be more satisfied with my vocation. She wasn't alarmed that my views and beliefs were evolving. Her beliefs were also changing.

"You are doing what they are supporting you to do. That is all that can be expected. What's going on in your mind is a private matter," she said.

As our return to Taiwan neared, I purchased theology and psychology books to help me in my journey. Bill, my former therapist, had introduced me to theology books that were considered liberal or heretical by my colleagues. I wanted to find a religious outlook that I could embrace, no matter what it was. I stretched my mind as much as possible. I wanted to feel something passionately again.

26

We returned to Taiwan, and I began to teach again at the Bible College. There were now only two missionary couples in Taiwan with our mission board: Arnie and his wife Debbie, and Kathy and me. So, this is where I was most needed. Plans for establishing a new church in Kaohsiung were shelved for the time being. I asked for courses that were more practical and less theological in nature, e.g., a course about the personal life of the minister. I enjoyed the challenge of presenting these courses in Chinese.

I prepared lectures in English and then gave the outline to our secretary, who translated them into Chinese. I then studied the outline and learned to use the Mandarin phraseology casually and extemporaneously. Classes were held in the evenings, so I was out three to four evenings each week. I returned each evening at 10:00 p.m. or later, tired but satisfied. I often stopped on the way home and brought candy bars for Kathy and me.

In the fall of 1989, our children were ready to start a new school year. We planned to send them to Morrison Academy. We trusted this to somehow work out financially. On one occasion during our furlough, we presented our program in a church in Tennessee which met in an office building. They were a start-up church with only twenty-five to thirty people in attendance.

At the end of the service, in front of the small congregation, the pastor asked us if we had any specific prayer requests as we were about to return to Taiwan. I said we were concerned about paying for our children's education in Taiwan.

"How much does it cost for one child?" the pastor asked as I stood before the congregation. I hesitated because the cost might sound exorbitant to many Americans.

"It is expensive," I said. But he pressed to know how much, and I reluctantly said that it was $3,000 per year for one child. Later that evening, as we packed up our things, the pastor approached me and handed me a check for $3,000. He said that the tiny church wanted to pay the tuition for one of our children for a year.

This pastor was actually bi-vocational, working as a schoolteacher during the week. The church didn't own a building, choosing rather to rent space in an office building on weekends. He said this approach enabled them financially to do things like they were doing for us.

Shortly after we arrived for our second term, Morrison Academy approached Kathy and asked if she might consider teaching third grade. The teacher who had been slated to teach had encountered an unexpected change of plans and was unable to teach.

"This is unbelievable!" Kathy said. "This is too good to be true." Not only would Kathy be paid to teach, but for each year she taught, one of our children received a significant discount on tuition. Not only would this solve our financial worries, but Kathy would also be a teacher, something she had put on hold when we began to have a family earlier than expected.

Kathy accepted the position, and we decided not to notify the mission board. We were pretty sure they would not approve the arrangement. If they found out, all we could say was that we had to educate our children. This was, in fact, the case.

"I'm going out in front of the house with the video camera and document the three of you headed out for the first day of school," I said. BR was in third grade and Margaret in first. A few days earlier, I helped Kathy get her classroom set up and decorated. Each morning after helping Kathy and the older two children off to school that fall, I saw Daniel off to a local Chinese kindergarten. One day, I put him in the little van that came to our house, and I spoke to the attendant, telling her that we wanted Daniel to stay the whole rather than half-day as usual. We sometimes did this if we had something to do in the afternoon.

"Noooooo, I don't want to stay all day." Daniel protested vehemently. Daniel hadn't been attending that long, so I thought I could say this in Mandarin without him understanding. He hated staying all day because they required him to take a nap. He said that the big room filled with tatamis smelled funny (probably a few bed-wetters).

Now it was quiet at home in the mornings, just me and Cinnamon, our toy poodle. Not long into our second term, Kathy said she heard about a place where we could get a pure-bred poodle puppy. Since we had given Shao Hei away before our furlough, I agreed that a puppy would be fun.

Bred by a Japanese breeder, his official name was "Ibushi Ibu." We decided on Cinnamon, and he became part of the family. Cinnamon went with me anytime I drove our van, his feet on the dashboard, looking back and forth as if scouting for danger. Sometimes when a neighbor heard me talking to him, they would say, "Oh, can he understand English?"

Kathy took the bus to Taipei once per month to take classes toward a master's degree. It was an extension program from Michigan State University. She took several classes before learning that the university would not recognize her undergraduate degree from Bob Jones University. She could not be a degree-seeking student. Kathy was disappointed but marshaled on, happy to be a teacher.

My trombone sat on its stand in the corner of the living room. We listened to an English radio station out of Taipei, and when a pop or jazz tune came on, I grabbed my trombone and played along. The head of the music department at Morrison Academy asked me to be an instructor for trombone and guitar a few hours each week. She was a cellist herself and a graduate of Bob Jones University who had gone on to study at the Eastman School of Music.

I organized a small combo with a few of the music teachers, sort of a Dixieland band. An American who had come to Taiwan to play cello in the Taiwan symphony played upright bass with us. We performed for the students and a few school functions.

As time passed and I didn't feel as constricted about my music choices, my love of jazz began to return. I had played in the jazz band for a while during high school. Later as I got into the religious scene, I ceased playing or listening to jazz. At BJU, jazz was considered worldly music and perhaps even evil. The style that jazz trombonists used, e.g., moving the slide rapidly to produce vibrato, was forbidden. We were taught to create vibrato with the control of breath and the embouchure.

Instrumental musicians are often described as either jazz players or legit players. Legit players are trained to play conventional music, usually classical. Even the best legit players in the world might find playing jazz confusing because the same music notation, when one is playing jazz, is played differently. The instruction I received at BJU was strictly legit.

A recital for the music faculty at Morrison Academy was planned, and I was to play a trombone solo. I chose for my performance the jazz ballad, "Stars Fell on Alabama." Rebecca, a young teacher who had recently graduated from the Eastman School of Music, accompanied me on piano. She was definitely a legit player, but we listened to a recording, and we did our best to emulate the style.

I'm sure my rendition wouldn't have earned any awards for jazz proficiency, but for that moment, I wasn't a fundamentalist missionary. I was a musician playing jazz.

***

"It makes more sense for you to be the pastor of the Lei Hu Church and for me to devote my time to overseeing the Bible College," Arnie said. Arnie carried a heavy burden overseeing the Bible College and serving as pastor of the church. He had been pressed into both roles due to the departure of other missionaries. Arnie had originally come to Taiwan to teach in the Bible College, so it made more sense for him to devote himself to this effort. The idea of me becoming pastor of Lei Hu Church appealed to me.

The Lei Hu Church functioned as the hub of our mission work in Taiwan. Various missionaries had served as pastor of the church at various times. I was to continue teaching at the Bible College but now devote much of my time to the work of church pastor.

The church made me an office out of a room above the sanctuary that had previously been an apartment. Carol, my assistant, was called *chuan dao*. This position was unique to Christian churches in Taiwan and is hard to translate into English. It literally means "person who spreads the message" but denotes a non-ordained worker in the church.

Carol helped with matters that involved more Chinese writing skills and other interactions with the membership where my cultural understanding was limited. In addition to preaching, I led the choir, met with the deacons, visited members and prospective members.

I presided over several weddings during my time as pastor there. Weddings were major events for a church in Taiwan. For such a ceremony, a couple stood at the front, facing the minister, the groom smiling broadly while the bride maintained an emotionless expression. It was a long service. For probably an hour, groups from various churches around the island came to the front and sang. It was not unlike a talent show. The Chinese have a term for this kind of atmosphere: *re nao*, which literally means hot-noisy.

In a traditional wedding, there was a feast during which the bride and groom went from table to table, toasting the guests. The Christian church weddings were sometimes followed by such a feast. Margaret's eyes grew wide with delight when she saw the bride change dresses several times, wearing various sequined *chi pao*, the slender traditional Chinese attire.

The Lei Hu Church planned a baptismal ceremony. Our own three children, now eleven, nine and seven were to be baptized. I had, at various times, talked to each of my children about accepting Christ as savior. I had led each of them in the prayer of inviting Jesus into their hearts to be their savior and take away their sins. Given all of our travels, there had never been a convenient time for them to be baptized. For me, as their father, to baptize them was special.

We conducted baptism by immersion which means the entire body is put under water briefly. This can sometimes be a little awkward, depending on the age and size of the person. Once I was asked by a student to come out to a remote church and perform several baptisms; the church was without a minister at the time. Reading maps in Chinese was not easy, and by the time I arrived, the service had already commenced. My student was in the choir and looked relieved when I came in and sat near the back.

I was concerned that I didn't see the baptistry, the tank of water that was used for the rite. In most churches, this was behind the pulpit, at a height where the congregants could observe. I began to feel nervous. I had never performed a baptism by any other method, such as sprinkling or pouring. I feared it might be awkward for me.

When the time for the baptism came, a couple of men moved the pulpit to the side, lifted up a sort of trap door and there was the baptistry under the pulpit. I hadn't seen this arrangement before. When I walked down the steps into the tank, the water was barely up to my knees, not waist deep as I expected. How was I going to completely immerse a person in such a small amount of water?

When a person is baptized, they really don't know what to expect, so when I pushed each person down into the shallow water, just enough to cover their face, I guess they accepted this as the way it was always done—and maybe it was at that church. I was later told that there was so little water because there was no drain, and they had to scoop it out after the ceremony.

On the day BR, Margaret and Daniel were to be baptized, several other people were also going to be baptized, including a young woman whom another member had brought to me saying that she had decided to become a Christian. I had led her in a prayer inviting Jesus into her life to save her soul. I told her about the upcoming baptism ceremony and encouraged her to come and be baptized.

When the day came, I baptized BR, Margaret and Daniel, along with several others. Kathy stood at the back of the church and beamed. Having grown up in church as she had, seeing her children being baptized by their father on the mission field was a thrill. Our children were following the beliefs that we had come to Taiwan to teach others.

As I was finishing the baptism portion of the service, I realized that the woman I had encouraged to be baptized had not come. I had spoken to her the day before, and everything was set. I changed into dry clothes as the choir sang and the offering was received.

I delivered the sermon, and as I concluded, the young woman came rushing in, looking frazzled. Transportation in Taiwan was by bus, motorcycle, or bicycle and she had encountered difficulty getting to the church.

"Is it too late?" she asked.

I changed back into my wet clothes and baptized her.

A few months later, Dr. Bob Jones Jr. visited Taiwan and was scheduled to speak at the Lei Hu Church. I jumped at the chance to interpret for such a famous preacher. He is among a few of the most eloquent preachers I have heard in my life. A trained Shakespearean actor, he has a tremendous grasp of the English language.

I stood beside Dr. Bob at the pulpit as he spoke a few sentences and waited for me to interpret his words into Mandarin. There is no time to ponder how to say something when interpreting in this manner. I had to be right on the heels of each phrase. Back in my BJU days, Dr. Bob could sometimes be harsh as he addressed religious trends of current events. But that day, he brought a gospel message in his fluid and dynamic style.

He took as his text the feeding of the five thousand with five loaves and two fishes. When he referred to the little boy's lunch, I translated this *bien dang*, the colloquial expression for the lunch boxes that children in Taiwan take to school each day. The congregants smiled. What a thrill it was to interpret his words into Chinese.

Yeh Nai Nai (Grandma Yeh) was the oldest mother at Lei Hu Church, nearly ninety years old. Her snow-white hair pulled into a bun on the back of her head reminded me of Granny. On Mother's Day, she cried, saying that she had not been a good daughter to her mother. Yeh Nai Nai was originally from Canton, China, where she had been a teacher. The Chinese have a joke about how difficult it is to understand a Cantonese person speaking Mandarin, and that was the case with Yeh Nai Nai.

Already short of stature, she was rather humped over and had only a few teeth. Her eyes, white with cataracts, appeared to go in opposite directions. When she said *Mai Mu Shi* (Pastor Mai), it sounded like *Mak bok Shi*, the Cantonese pronunciation.

Our Chinese name, Mai, is pronounced *Mak* in Cantonese. While not common in Taiwan, the surname is quite common in Canton. One day, a thought came to me. *I wonder if Yeh Nai Nai knows that I am not Chinese.* She could hardly see at all and my name sounded very familiar to that of a Cantonese person. Often after church, she took the five of us and treated us to beef-noodle soup with an egg in it. Maybe for my children, being with Yeh Nai Nai felt like I felt when I was with Granny.

27

Dr. Decker was a retired Presbyterian minister who specialized in pastoral counseling. He had come to Taiwan to help the missionary community. I started going to see him each week. This was helpful in many ways, and he didn't charge for this service.

"You can prove anything from the Bible," he said one day. While not really a profound statement, it really struck me. The rigid doctrine I had been taught was, in fact, one among many ways of explaining the Bible, a book filled with often contradictory statements. Dr. Decker could address theological issues, though he came from a more moderate denominational background.

I continued taking counseling courses via distance learning. The concept of therapy took a lot of explaining to the local people. It wasn't a part of society. At one point, Arnie and I thought it a good idea to give me the title "Director of Counseling" at the Bible College. Students who had problems could come to talk with me. No one ever availed themselves of this. We later learned the Chinese word posted on my door meant the person to see if you had gotten in some kind of trouble in school—oops.

Kathy and I had begun to branch out and become friends with missionaries other than those on our mission board. I became friends with George. He had actually considered himself a fundamentalist when he first came to Taiwan as a missionary but had grown disaffected with that designation. George also suffered from

depression, and we both benefitted from jogging. He and I often met
to pound the pavement in the sweltering Taiwan heat.

Greg was with another fundamentalist group. He was tall, 6
ft. 6 in., and large of heart. Like me, Greg had found himself in an
ultra-conservative mission group and felt uncomfortable with it. He
and I hit it off from the start. We often met for a steamed bun before
playing tennis together. Always jovial, he was an interesting sight in
a country of relatively short people—a huge hairy man riding on a
Vespa scooter. I looked forward to our matches.

I went about my duties as pastor and teacher and led activities
for the church with diligence, trying to ignore my reservations, not
only about ultra-conservative Christianity but about Christianity
in general. If it wasn't exclusionary—declaring all who didn't
believe are damned to hell—I could accept the basic teachings of
Christianity, i.e., God sent his son to save us from our sins, wants us
to experience an abundant life, love your neighbor as yourself, etc.
Despite my inner conflict, I think I was good at being a pastor, and
people expressed appreciation for my work among them. Attendance
at the church increased.

The issue of ancestor worship proved a huge obstacle to a
person considering becoming a Christian. In order for a person to
be cared for in the afterlife, family members must engage in certain
rituals after their death. It was common to see tables filled with food,
fruit, even beer, set in front of a home with incense burning around
it. This was to provide for ancestors in the afterlife.

There were stores that sold bundles of spirit money (not actual
currency, sometimes called "hell money") to be burned in front of
one's home as part of ancestor worship, presumably to provide for
relatives in the afterlife. There were certain days based on the lunar
calendar when such worship was to take place.

Male offspring were expected to worship their parents and
other ancestors. If a person converted to Christianity, the expectation
was to cease these practices, thus refusing to fulfill a basic filial

responsibility to one's parents and forebears. For this reason, it was especially consequential for a man to decide to become a Christian.

One day I received a letter from a college classmate who was now a missionary in Japan. He had read one of our newsletters in which I had talked about a home gathering one month following a church member's death. This was customary for the Chinese and, to me, was like a memorial service. My friend and fellow missionary expressed surprise and concern that I had participated in such a ceremony. In his thinking, this related to ancestor worship. He cautioned me against participating in this practice.

I never answered the letter, not because I felt I had done anything wrong but because I really had ceased to have any common point of reference with which to discuss this with him or others of like mind. I comforted someone who was grieving, nothing more. I didn't care to engage in some biblical search of relevant teachings.

Now, I couldn't muster the will to combat my questions. Doubts about my faith came regularly. I couldn't hold them off. The wall that I had constructed to keep them at bay was crumbling. Like the boy with his finger in the hole of the dike, I had dared to remove the defenses and entertain questions. The wall was crumbling, and a torrent of other doubts washed over me.

Why do I seem to think differently from my colleagues, seeing things as more intricate and complex than others see them? When a non-believer expressed skepticism about the possibility of one true God, I couldn't glibly repeat the apologetics and defenses that I had learned. The reservations that such a person had were, to me, worthy of respect. *Is this some kind of special capacity I had to empathize with others, or a flaw in my faith?*

Important to fundamentalism is the "inspiration and inerrancy of scripture." For years, I suppressed skepticism about this. There are contradictions in the Bible that are difficult to accept, if not preposterous. Samson was said to have killed one thousand Philistines with the jawbone of an ass. How could this have actually happened? Would the Philistines have lined up and waited their turn to be beaten to death with a bone? In order to secure the hand of Michal, the king's daughter, in marriage, David presented the foreskins of two hundred Philistines to King Saul (I Samuel 18:27). If such a thing actually happened, I seriously doubt the foreskins were surgically removed.

The following verse is cited when teaching the doctrine of the inspiration of scripture: "All scripture is given by inspiration of God, and is profitable for doctrine, for reproof, for correction, for instruction in righteousness" (II Timothy 3:16). Paul was referring to the Hebrew scriptures, what Christians call the "Old Testament." It couldn't have been referring to the "New Testament," which wasn't compiled until much later.

In a way, this teaching (inerrancy of scripture) serves to ensure that some people will never embrace the Christian faith. A person might find the faith appealing and comforting in many respects, but to have to accept everything in the Bible as valid, to be embraced regardless of reservations, is something many are not willing to do.

For so long, I believed that I had been *called* to pursue this life of ministry. What was I originally called to do? Was it to proclaim that one must believe a certain way in order to avoid going to hell? Or was it to help people, and this Christian message was the vehicle available to me, a boy from Alabama?

***

Driving up the winding road, we were aware of going higher and higher into the mountains, but it was too dark to fully take in our surroundings. It was late by the time we arrived at the hostel where we would spend the night. Kathy and I wanted to get away for a couple of days, and someone had recommended this little place in the mountains of Taiwan. BR, Margaret and Daniel stayed with missionary friends. By now, we were used to exploring remote places and sites, our Mandarin was adequate to navigate what we encountered.

We slept late the next morning, no children waking us asking for breakfast. We awoke to a breathtaking mountain vista from our room's window. The sun was already up above the horizon, and a mist arose from the landscape in the foreground. We quickly dressed and headed out to begin exploring.

On the street, people scurried about, some on bicycles, a few on motor scooters. Venders selling clothing or toys were setting up their mats. A woman struggled under the weight of a pole across her shoulders, baskets at each end filled with produce. Two men squatted, playing a game, their lips red from chewing betel nut.

Our plan was to grab something to eat on our way. Breakfast was typically readily available and cheap. A steamed bun, maybe some hot soymilk with a deep-fried grease stick. It was common for housewives to set up little tables on the street or lane and sell what they had made that morning. Maybe we would find some "shao long bao," a sort of dumpling steamed in bamboo baskets, one of our favorites.

By now, it was almost 10:00 a.m., and all of the breakfast vendors seemed to have packed up for the day. A teenage girl tended a stand selling Star Fruit drink (Carambola), big transparent vats containing the odd-shaped yellow-green fruit stood at each end of her booth. Expecting that young people usually had good Mandarin, we asked her to recommend a path to explore the mountains. She giggled, amused to be talking to foreigners, and pointed to a path ahead behind a flower stand. We set out on a well-worn trail leading away from the village.

The air was fresh and clean, so different from the ever-present exhaust smells of Taichung. We were sure that we would come across someone selling something to eat, a least a "tea egg," always sold anywhere there were people.

We made our way along a gradually narrowing trail, taking in the natural scenery. There were terraced vegetable gardens on the hillsides. An occasional rooster crowed. The path narrowed, and as we rounded a bend, we came upon a little building. We could see into a screened-in area and saw several round tables with plastic chairs. "Great! A restaurant." Kathy said.

We opened the door and walked in. A woman, perhaps in her early thirties, stood at a sink washing some cooking utensils. She looked like other women we often saw in the area, her hair pinned in a bun on her head, neat but not stylish clothes, rubber sandals, no make-up of any kind. A child, not much more than a year old, played at her feet. She wiped her hands on her apron and looked at us inquisitively, probably surprised to be encountering foreigners.

We spoke to her in Mandarin, and she appeared to understand, but we couldn't understand her response. Other languages and dialects are common in rural areas. We asked if this was a restaurant. She shook her head from side to side, indicating it was not. As she said something that we couldn't understand, she pointed to one of the tables in a welcoming way. *If it isn't a restaurant, why is she inviting us to sit?*

She put her child in a sling on her back and began cooking what looked like scrambled eggs with green onions. She gave us a little plate of peanuts and dried seaweed, along with a bowl of warm bean curd milk. In a jar on the table were chopsticks and a few spoons.

After finishing our breakfast, we asked how much we owed. But as best we could understand, she indicated there was no charge. We insisted that we pay, but she was adamant. We thought this was odd, but all we could do was express our gratitude, which we did, bowing slightly in the Chinese manner, thanking her earnestly. We left and continued on our adventure.

We hadn't walked very far when the path turned sharply, and suddenly before us stood an impressive, colorful structure. It was obviously a temple, called a "miao" in Mandarin. Usually, such rural temples have at the focal point of the pavilion-like structure the image of a red-faced warrior, incense sticks burning around it.

Religion in Taiwan is a mixture of Taoism, Buddhism and ancestor worship. Small temples like this are scattered about the landscape, especially in rural areas.

At the center of this temple was a sight we hadn't seen before, a life-size statue of a woman with many arms coming out of her shoulders, quite a startling image the first time one sees it. Her arms reached out in many directions. This is a sort of female Buddha known by various names. In Taiwan, it is often referred to as "Guan Yin" (Kuan Yin), which translates roughly as "the one who perceives the sounds of the world." Some depictions of Guan Yin show each hand with an eye in her palm. This personage, signifying compassion and care, varies from place to place throughout Asia.

As Christian missionaries, we usually did not visit such places of worship, rather observing only from a distance. After all, we were in Taiwan to teach the truth. Suddenly it dawned on me the connection between the two structures we had just seen. The restaurant-like building where we had eaten was for followers of Guan Yin, where they had their meals when making their pilgrimage to this temple. The woman who had cooked our breakfast was there to cook for such people.

We continued on our way, taking in new sights and sounds. But I couldn't stop pondering the peculiar irony of what we had just experienced. We had been the recipients of kindness and hospitality by this worker at this retreat center for adherents of a different belief system, one that our faith structure considered false. If I had known what the purpose of the place was, I probably wouldn't have entered.

I added this to the ever-deepening repository of thoughts and questions that grew within me as I learned of and experienced this land and culture so different from all that I had previously known. This humble woman, most likely minimally educated, with whom we could communicate only with difficulty, had shown us kindness, accepting nothing in return. We were here as messengers of the truth, but what truth?

Other evangelical missionaries would no doubt have immediately identified this as a religion of a false god. They might have been amused by the odd image, maybe even taken a photo of it, but would have had no difficulty concluding that this affirmed their (our) reason for being here, to proclaim the message of the true God. But, I just couldn't stop thinking about the woman who was so kind to us, that how this was what she had known from childhood, not unlike our reason for believing what we believed.

The weekend trip had been worthwhile. Kathy and I enjoyed our time together. The natural beauty and fresh air in the mountains were restorative. The experience with the breakfast and the temple seemed to have nudged me yet another step toward altering the way I viewed life and the world.

***

Sweat poured off us as we walked in the sweltering heat of Singapore in March 1992. Everyone there had on shorts and sandals. Our family of five was visiting at the invitation of a church that was theologically similar to the Lei Hu Church.

Singapore is a city-state with a population of five million; roughly 75 percent ethnic Chinese, with the remainder of the population split mostly between people of Indian or Malaysian descent. Positioned at the bottom tip of the Malay Peninsula, it is slightly north of the equator. English is widely spoken, along with Mandarin Chinese, and a number of other languages and dialects.

This tiny country has jokingly been referred to as a *fine city* because of the strict laws and the many things you can be fined for doing: spitting in public, failing to flush a public toilet, or walking around nude in your own house. Chewing gum is banned from the entire country. It is, in fact, a very clean and pleasant place to visit, albeit very hot.

There was another purpose for this trip. We had become good friends with Rahn and his wife, who were affiliated with a particular missionary organization that interested us. The missionaries in this group pursued their own sense of calling. This group could be considered evangelical—they emphasized proclaiming the death and resurrection of Christ, personal conversion, belief in a straightforward reading of the Bible—but they were not fundamentalist. They were much more inclusive in their approach, willing to work in tandem with established denominations. By affiliating with this group, we thought we could continue to be missionaries in Taiwan.

Rahn's mission organization planned a meeting of their leaders in Singapore at the time of our visit, and they agreed to meet with Kathy and me. We had already gone through a few steps of applying to the organization prior to the trip.

God, is this your hand at work, making it possible for us to affiliate with a different organization? We were in Singapore under the pretense of being fundamentalist missionaries while at the same time interviewing for an affiliation with a non-fundamentalist group. I felt as if I were trying to be two different persons at once, quite a psychological strain. But, ever the gregarious and charming person I've been told I can be—someone once said I could charm the leaves off a tree—it is unlikely that anyone noticed.

The organization leaders liked us and our plan to have a counseling ministry in Taiwan, but they were not sure it fit with their particular mission model and philosophy. It took some convincing on our part that a couple having both attended Bob Jones University could be comfortable with their more inclusive approach. They suggested we attend one of their conferences back in the US and explore further whether our mission objectives were compatible with theirs.

After returning from Singapore, we began to back away from pursuing Rahn's mission group. I found another mission board that would clear funds for us for a while as associate missionaries. This felt like a great leap forward. I decided to inform the Lei Hu Church that we intended to resign and leave Taiwan sometime in June. As their pastor, I felt I owed them this advance information. We told them our plan to return to Taiwan in a different missionary capacity.

In reality, there was no need to rush this change, but I had become so unhappy that the strain felt crippling. We constantly received memos from our organization criticizing the endeavors of other mission groups, and I was friends with the missionaries of these groups. This made me feel unclean, as though I was wearing disease-infested clothing that I must shed as quickly as possible.

I sat in our living room, the pressure of making this leap weighing heavily on me. I picked up my trombone and played through the scales and arpeggios I had learned during my earlier studies. The order and symmetry of the exercises calmed me. The feel of the instrument in my hands, along with its mellow sound, still gave me a warm, reassuring feeling.

We discussed our tentative plans with Arnie and Debbie. They were sympathetic to our discontent, even if they did not necessarily hold our same religious views. They were good and loyal friends, and we trusted them.

We knew there was a chance that our plans could get back to our mission board in the US. A few former Bible College students had gone to the states to continue studies at BJU. Word travels fast, even to the other side of the world.

The board got wind of our plans and told us to leave Taiwan by June 1.

Part V
Divided Mind

28

The trees showed the beginnings of yellows and oranges as I drove along the Virginia roadway. There it was—the exit I was looking for—Nellysford, Virginia. I drove for a while on a two-lane road. Fields on either side, occasionally a few cows or a horse, split rail fences. Old barns dotted the landscape.

Ahead, sitting up on a hill, was Rockfish Valley Baptist Church. I pulled into the gravel driveway and parked shy of the cemetery, which wrapped around the back of the church. I was early for the service, so I settled in to wait, looking over my sermon for the day.

In September 1992, we lived in Lynchburg, Virginia. When a neighbor asked me if I could fill the pulpit for her sister's church in a small town one hour north of Lynchburg, I agreed. The pay was one hundred dollars. I didn't come to Lynchburg to be a preacher, but I couldn't afford to turn down the offer.

The church was in a picturesque area, not far from the town upon which the book and televisions series *The Waltons* was based. After that Sunday, they offered another one hundred dollars to come on Wednesday evening to lead the Bible study.

We didn't know anyone in Lynchburg except one professor at Liberty University. Dr. Miller had been my psychology professor at BJU years before, though, at the time, I really had no personal interaction with him nor much interest in psychology. His wife had been the OB nurse at the hospital when BR was born and taught the pre-natal classes we attended.

I corresponded with Dr. Miller from Taiwan, and he and his wife offered to help us find a place to live. He thought he could get me a job as a graduate assistant at Liberty University. Dr. and Mrs. Miller had left BJU because the university deemed him not fundamentalist enough. More than most, they understood what we were attempting to do. They said they admired our courage.

After an emotional departure from Taiwan, we spent a month in Mobile visiting family before moving to Lynchburg, so I could complete my master's degree in counseling in residence at Liberty University.

We had found a missionary family who wanted to rent our house in Taiwan, furnished. After finishing the degree, we would need to raise more financial support under the new mission board before returning to Taiwan. We hoped to return to Taiwan in one or two years.

My parents gave us a car they no longer needed, and we purchased an inexpensive second car and headed for Virginia in August. We enrolled the children in public school, and Kathy found a job working as an assistant helping students who were struggling academically. The job for me as a teaching assistant didn't pan out, at least not at first.

A church donated some old furniture and pots and pans. We didn't have a table to eat at for a few weeks until we found a cheap one at a used furniture store. The house backed up to woods, and we often saw raccoons and deer. Cinnamon, who had returned from Taiwan with us, once took off after some deer, and it took us several hours to find him. We barely scraped by. BR, age thirteen, followed me around like a puppy, so lonely without any friends. I put up a basketball goal for him in the backyard so we could play together.

Preaching at the little country church turned into a regular gig, twice a week for a few months. The church members were content to have me as their interim pastor. A consistent preacher at the little church boosted the church attendance, which, without a pastor, had dwindled down to twelve to fifteen people. One Sunday, I took my banjo and played along with the choir of four people.

"Brother preacher, can you bring that banjo again next Sunday?" one elderly man said, looking at the instrument adoringly. Once, our whole family performed before the church, each playing an instrument. BR on trombone, Margaret on saxophone, me on trombone and Kathy on the piano. Daniel played a drum.

The scenery was more beautiful with each passing week that fall as I made the drive into the Virginia mountains. On Wednesdays, I listened to National Public Radio as I drove. The familiar introductory music to *All Things Considered* became a welcome companion. This was so refreshing and enjoyable because various viewpoints were presented without dogmatism or acrimony.

Finally, the job as a teaching assistant came through. I graded papers for the distance-learning program. It was a good job since I could fit it in around my classes. I poured myself into my studies— psychology, not theology. I let my hair grow a little longer, along with the beard I already had.

On the drive to the church one Sunday morning, I stopped to fill my tank with gas. I was still not used to some of the ways gas pumps had changed during our years in Taiwan. I put the hose in my tank, lifted the handle and selected the fuel I wanted. Nothing happened. Then I saw a round button that said, "To begin pumping, press here." When I pushed that button, the hose came out of the tank as if shot from a rocket. It hit the ground, and a stream of gasoline shot right at me. Before I knew what was happening, I was drenched.

"Bruthah Macdoner, I sme-ul ga-is," one of the men in the church said as I readied the sanctuary for worship. I hadn't had time to go home and change clothes. It dried by the time I got to church, but the odor had not gone away. I saw people wrinkling their noses and looking around in search of the odor's source. I didn't tell anyone what had happened. I silently prayed no one would strike a match.

.   At the country church, I had no duties other than preaching, and I didn't really mind it. I have always been good with older people, which made up most of those at the little church. I tried to be sincere in what I preached. This limited my topics since I had come to question much of what Christians believe.

The Wednesday evening Bible study was small. Two aging ladies always came together and were fun to be around. We called them the Baldwin Sisters referencing *The Waltons*. One night, one of the Baldwin sisters talked about visiting her aged mother in a nursing home the previous day.

"I sang her a little song. I think she enjoyed it," she shared with a slight sob.

"As only a mother could," the other woman quipped.

People in that part of Virginia had certain words they pronounced in a distinct way. "House" was hoos. "About" sounded like aboot. One night I observed one of the Baldwin sisters didn't speak in this manner, but I knew they were both from the area.

"How come you don't say aboot the hoos like she does?" I asked.

"She's just trying to show off," the other said.

I am good at being a pastor to people like this. Why can't I just accept the Christian faith, lock, stock and barrel as so many others do? To me, it came back to compassion and fairness. As much as the Christian faith taught that everyone had a chance, it was clear to me that this wasn't true. Even for those who grew up in America, it didn't always resonate with certain people, at least not in the born-again approach emphasized by evangelicals.

29

I enjoyed my studies at Liberty. We explored theories of personality and approaches to therapy from both secular and Christian standpoints. Jerry Falwell, the founder and president of Liberty University, was a nationally known political conservative, having founded and run the Moral Majority during the 1980s. I usually worked during chapel and thus avoided hearing him. I had begun to feel an aversion for American evangelicalism and the conservative politics that went along with it. Warnings that liberalism or humanism were ruining America didn't resonate with me anymore.

Liberty University tried to maintain a conservative emphasis while at the same time gaining respect among secular universities. They did not use the term fundamentalist. They preferred conservative, which had a less negative connotation. They had a football team, coached by a former NFL coach, and a marching band. Students had a lot more freedom than students at BJU. Liberty allowed religious music considered Christian Rock, anathema at my alma mater.

Many students in the counseling program had come to study at Liberty because they wanted a Christian approach. Because Liberty was an accredited university preparing students to become licensed mental health professionals, mainstream secular theories of counseling were also taught.

Now thirty-seven years old, I was older than nearly all of my classmates—and some of my professors. Though a pastor on weekends, I remained skeptical about a so-called Christian approach to counseling. I had walked away from the narrowness of the fundamentalism in which I had been trapped for so long, and I refused to accept any dogmatic religious views.

My turn to secular psychology had taken place when the pat formulas espoused by Christianity had not worked for me. I was skeptical of any view that purported to adhere to a biblical standard. The professors were thorough, and I learned a great deal.

We settled into our new surroundings. BR tried out for football at his middle school, something he had seen only on television. He proved a natural athlete and picked up sports quickly. During one game, he intercepted a pass. Excited, he did what he had seen on the videotapes of football games. He spiked the ball right in the middle of the field. As a result, his team was penalized for delay of game.

Margaret became friends with a little girl her age who lived on our street. They became inseparable. One thing about living in so many places is that our children made friends easily. Daniel played video games—Nintendo or Sega Genesis. One day an elderly man knocked on our door. At first, I didn't recognize him, but then I realized he was our neighbor. He played jazz organ and he and I had jammed once or twice.

"Is Daniel home?" he asked. *Why does he want Daniel?* "I wanted to see if Daniel wants to swap video game cartridges."

The gig at the country church ran out in January when the church called a full-time pastor. The two hundred dollars per week had been vital to us. We needed to find another source of income.

***

I was invited to fill the pulpit at a Chinese church in Virginia Beach, a three-hour drive from Lynchburg. Kathy and I relished a nice getaway, so we left the children with friends and drove there for the weekend. I wasn't familiar with Chinese churches in America.

I preached two times, once for the English-speaking service (the younger members of the congregation) and again for the Chinese-speaking service. We stayed in a room on the oceanfront, the waves of the Atlantic Ocean breaking right outside the hotel window. We walked on the beach and picked up shells.

My ability to speak Chinese impressed the church, and they were pleased that one speaker could cover both services. They invited me to come again to preach a month later. We ended up making the trip to Virginia Beach several times that spring. The honorariums helped, but it was a long drive.

On one of our visits to the church, we attended what we thought was a social gathering at the home of one of the church members. All of the church elders and deacons were present, and they were considering me as a candidate to become their full-time pastor. I didn't take this seriously at first. After all, I didn't want to be a pastor anymore.

Back in Lynchburg, I continued the rigorous pace of taking classes, working as a teaching assistant, and preaching in churches on weekends when I could. I also served an internship in counseling during that spring semester, working several nights per week at the university counseling center.

As the conclusion of the semester approached, I prepared to take my comprehensive exams and complete my master's degree. But now, I also considered the invitation to move to Virginia Beach to become pastor of First Chinese Baptist Church. I needed a job come June, and this church offered one.

The older children, BR, age fourteen, and Margaret, twelve, had participated in the youth program at Thomas Road Baptist Church in Lynchburg, where Jerry Falwell served as pastor. It had a big youth program, and we thought this was important for their acclimation back to life in America. Kathy and I only attended the church a few times. I was nearly always away on weekends preaching, and Kathy visited various churches when not accompanying me.

My studies fast came to a conclusion. I received a master's degree in counseling in May 1993. My parents came for yet another ceremony.

On Mother's Day, we ate lunch at a Chinese restaurant, and I pulled out the slip of paper inside my fortune cookie. "You will be chosen for a position of great honor." I waited for the call from the church in Virginia Beach.

They voted to call me as pastor, with all but one vote in favor. "Even if the candidate had been Jesus, that person would likely have opposed it," the church leader said when relaying to me the result of the vote. The call was for one year since we had told them of our plans to return to Taiwan.

"Whatever," BR said, using the teen-speak he had picked up. "We move every year anyway." The children had barely settled into life in Lynchburg when we moved again. Margaret cried during the entire trip to Virginia Beach. She didn't want to leave her best friend.

I felt terrible about doing this to the children again but saw no other path for us at the time. They were about to attend their third school in as many years. We did our best to be upbeat and make the best of it. Kathy, always willing to rise to the occasion, embraced the move and began researching which neighborhoods in Virginia Beach had the best schools. We loaded up a rental truck and headed to our new home.

30

God, is it your plan for me to be a pastor despite my desire to do otherwise? Is your call indeed irrevocable?

We chose to live in an area where the schools were considered better academically but also had good music and band programs. BR started ninth grade and immediately became involved in the marching band. He attended summer marching band rehearsals almost immediately. Margaret would attend middle school and Daniel elementary school. New schools, new friends, yet again.

Our new home had a pond in the back that bordered several houses. Cinnamon became obsessed with the ducks in the pond. For the first few days, he could be seen swimming furiously behind a duck, trying to catch it, the duck paddling leisurely to stay ahead of him. After a few such efforts, he ignored the ducks.

We didn't totally understand what it meant to become a part of the Chinese-American community. We had immersed ourselves into the local culture to a significant degree in Taiwan, but this was a little different. The people in Taiwan usually viewed us as a novelty, foreigners who could speak Chinese. They wanted to meet us and learn from us. These immigrants in the US tried to maintain their Chinese culture and language. Our role in this was unclear.

The children of these immigrants were quite Americanized, and most had little interest in learning Chinese or maintaining Chinese customs. Their parents didn't know what to make of us. On the one hand, we admired Chinese culture and could speak their language, something that they wished for their children. But, on the other hand, we were Americans and largely thought and acted like Americans. It was understandable that as immigrants, they were cautious about their children totally embracing American culture.

BR became active in the youth program of a church similar to the one he and Margaret had attended in Lynchburg, but Margaret didn't seem to take to it. She and Daniel tried to participate more in the children's and youth program of the First Chinese Baptist Church, where I served as pastor. BR tried to participate in both churches.

The only job Kathy could find was one of a telemarketer, cold-calling people in the evenings and asking them to allow a salesman to visit them to sell them a funeral plot. Later, she got a part-time job as a reading instructor in the public schools.

For a while, Kathy worked as a teacher in a women's prison, teaching inmates working on a GED while incarcerated. She had started a master's degree in education while in Lynchburg and, for the next couple of years, made a monthly three-hour drive to continue this program. She eventually became the Director of Adult and Continuing Education for the City of Virginia Beach.

I dove into my role as pastor. I tried to view my intellectual reservations as a natural part of my development and not inappropriate for a pastor who was well educated and thoughtful. The mainstream evangelical world that we had encountered in Lynchburg, while quite conservative in the big picture, was a move to the left compared with our years associated with BJU. After all, presidents Carter and Clinton were both Southern Baptists.

First Chinese Baptist had been established by Baptists in 1901 and was affiliated with the Southern Baptist Convention. While some certainly view Southern Baptists as conservative, it was a move back to my roots. I hoped to embrace mainstream evangelicalism and be content with my faith outlook and role as a pastor in this setting.

I was the pastor of three distinct groups of people in the church. The first were recent immigrants, mostly from Taiwan, many of whom were professors at local universities. Some had been Christians in Taiwan before coming to the US.

A second group was the *Toisanese* people. These were Chinese who had come to the US beginning in the early 1900s. They were shopkeepers and restaurateurs, some even having been born in the US. A number had served in the US military. They spoke a different dialect, but most could speak English. The *Toisanese* had come from a poor part of China. Unlike the later Chinese immigrants who were college-educated and came to the US to attend graduate school, they had come desperate to find a better life. Some had come illegally and had managed to stay and become model citizens.

Johnson Wong told me he originally came under false papers, using another person's name. This was common in the 1940s and 50s. As a twelve-year-old, he was put in first grade. There was no instruction for non-English speakers. The next year he leaped up to fourth grade and then to middle school and eventually high school. He proudly graduated from high school, though he never spoke English without a heavy accent. When World War II broke out, he was drafted into the US military.

"When I went into the Army, I couldn't speak English very well. When I got out, I had almost forgotten how to speak Chinese," he told me, chuckling. "When I was in the Army, I still used the paper name that I used to get into America. Later on, the US government said we could all go back to our real names."

"I heard that you were in the Normandy Invasion, D-Day. Is that true?" I asked him one day.

"Yea, I was," he said in his humble manner.

"That must have been awful!" I said.

"It wasn't too bad," he said. "Most of the bad fighting was up ahead of us."

During the time that I was pastor in Virginia Beach, I conducted a dozen or more funerals for many of these early Chinese immigrants to the US. Often, an American flag was presented at the graveside to their loved ones for service to their country.

The third type of church member was what we called the A-B-Cs (American-born Chinese). This usually referred to the younger generation born in the US and who could not speak Chinese, at least very little. For them, we held a separate service each Sunday. They preferred a more American style of worship with the singing of contemporary English songs and choruses. The church leaders saw me as a perfect pastor because I could communicate with and relate to these members who had grown up in America.

Organizing church activities that included all three groups was challenging. We had to deal with three languages, Mandarin, Toisanese, and English. I did my best to navigate all the language borders.

I needed a couple of additional classes to qualify for a counseling license in Virginia, so I decided to take a class at William & Mary, an hour away in Williamsburg. I stood back and looked at the sticker I had affixed to the bumper of my car. *The College of William & Mary, 300 years, 1693–1993.* I could possibly have found something closer in Norfolk, but I wanted to study at this historic university, where there was no expectation of conformity to any religious ideology. The small act of attaching a campus parking sticker on my car felt liberating.

In 1994 Kathy and I returned to Taiwan to close up our home and bring back what we could of our belongings. Everything indicated it was God's will that I be the pastor of the Chinese church in Virginia. We accepted this.

We sorted through belongings and decided what to give away, throw away, or pack to ship back to the US. There was a twelve-hour time difference, and we could barely hold our eyes open. But we had no time to sleep it off. I just laid down on the floor of the empty house to sleep for a few minutes before continuing to pack.

Each item in our Taiwan home brought back a flood of memories. Chinese language study books, pieces of the local furniture that we had used, the steel propane tanks that fueled our water heater and kitchen stove, knick-knacks that had been given to us by our Chinese friends. With each decision about an item, I felt as though I couldn't take any more, a dark mass swelling ever larger in my chest.

Kathy and I stood in the kitchen and stared at the wall where we had marked the children's heights during the seven years we had lived there. They were six, four and two when we had arrived in Taiwan in 1985. When we left in 1992, they were thirteen, eleven and nine. We marked their heights each year, careful to preserve that portion of the wall when we repainted. Kathy used a large piece of paper and copied every mark and every notation so that we could take it back to our home in Virginia, where it hangs today.

Kathy returned to the US after a week, and I stayed another week to arrange for a shipping container and to oversee packing it. My old pal Greg knew some mountain people who were in the moving business, and they came to pack the container. Three muscular, bare-chested, barefoot young men arrived at our house. After a brief survey of what was involved, they suggested a price, I agreed, and they began.

One carried a full-sized filing cabinet (full of papers) down three flights of stairs on his back. Another carried the refrigerator. Two men moved our piano by using a strap which they put around their shoulders and under the piano, and walked out the door seemingly with little effort.

It was blisteringly hot in the house. The air-conditioners had been sold. One of the young men, stationed in the metal container, carefully packed each item. It could easily have been 120 degrees in there, and sweat poured off him, but he worked as if this made little difference.

I had arranged to meet our old landlord to settle up. The house was new ten years ago when we first rented it. Over the years, Mr.

Yeh occasionally came down to Taichung from Taipei and arrived at our house on a bicycle from the bus station. Mr. Yeh was a gentle little man with a wisp of white hair that always revolted against the efforts of a comb. As he talked, he periodically tried to put it back into place. He always spoke as if he were apologizing or was embarrassed to say whatever he had to say. When we initially rented the house, we had to work through a translator. Now, we can speak freely in Mandarin.

Ten years earlier, we had given him a security deposit of $375. I counted on getting it back. When I asked Mr. Yeh about this, he responded in his somewhat apologetic manner that customarily, this money was not returned to the renter.

"Ah, Old Yeh, Mr. Mai has been a good tenant. He has taken good care of your house. You couldn't have found local tenants who were so conscientious. You should give him his key money!" my neighbor piped up. He had been on the other side of the fence listening.

I don't know why my neighbor went to bat for me, except that when his brother-in-law had applied to an American university for study years before, I had assisted him by talking to the admissions office on the phone. It is a peculiar thing, but when you help a Chinese person, they will diligently search for a way to return the favor, even if it takes years.

At this point, Mr. Yeh would have lost face to have refused to return my deposit, so he agreed. He really didn't seem to mind too much. I was lucky his wife was not there. She drove a much harder bargain.

A truck came and pulled the container away. I walked down the lane from the house as I had done hundreds of times. My heart completely lodged in my throat. I wanted to cry but couldn't. So many important things had happened at this house. I didn't look back. I walked to the home of Arnie and Debbie, our dear fellow missionary colleagues.

31

Back in Virginia, the church grew in numbers. Each year at the meeting of the local Baptist association, we received recognition for church growth. We usually had a baptism service on Easter Sunday. Once I baptized fifteen people in one service. I believed faith in Christ could bring peace and direction to a person's life, though I still couldn't accept the teaching that non-Christians were condemned to hell. I don't know whether or not church members noticed that I never talked about hell as the fate of non-believers. I suspect some wished for me to say more about this but probably did not guess that I did not believe it.

I realized various factors came into play in these individuals' decision to become Christians. Some of the recent immigrants found in the Chinese church a community that spoke their language and enabled them to feel at home. It was also, for them, a way of casting off the superstitions of their country of origin, or the atheism in the case of communist China, and to transition to what they felt was a new and better life philosophy, and possibly because they believed it was American.

I continued to prepare myself for something else. I applied and was accepted into the Ed.S. program at the College of William and Mary (thirty hours beyond a master's degree). I could likely have found a similar program at one of the several universities nearer

to where we lived, but I wanted to have a degree from William &
Mary, a school I didn't have to apologize for.

I took a graduate course nearly every semester for the seven
years I was pastor of the church, completing the coursework for a
Ph.D. in counseling which I received a few years after leaving the
area.

For so long, I had lived in a religious world where what you
said or the viewpoint you held was scrutinized as to whether it
conformed to evangelical religious teachings. Any learning that did
not promote salvation was, at best, superfluous.

"What good is it to fill a man's stomach if his soul is going to burn
for eternity in hell?" Such statements were staples in fundamentalist
sermons. Ironically the Bible, in at least one well-known passage,
says almost the opposite: ". . . and one of you say unto them, depart
in peace, be ye warmed and filled; notwithstanding ye give them not
those things which are needful to the body; What doeth it profit?"
(James 2:16)

The classes at William & Mary were so refreshing to me because
people were open-minded and not dogmatic about the answers to
life's perplexities. It is ironic that I had gravitated to Christianity
earlier in life because it offered clear answers at a time in my life
when the world felt confusing to me. Once I admitted to myself
that my problems and those of the world could not be solved by
simply following Bible prescriptions, the evangelical script became
loathsome to me.

On the way home from classes in Williamsburg, I sometimes
stopped in Norfolk and rehearsed with a brass group that needed a
trombone player. I performed with them on one or two occasions. I
formed a Dixie-land group, including the high school band director
and a few other musicians I met locally. These opportunities
somewhat satisfied my longing to continue playing music.

I set up an extra room in our house as a sort of music studio. I
had a cheap set of drums and an electric guitar from my childhood.

I bought a microphone and a small amplifier, and Daniel learned to play the bass guitar. "O-O-O listen to the music, O-O-O-O-O listen to the music." BR on the drums, me singing and playing guitar, and Daniel on bass; we tried to play the oldies and a few newer pop tunes. We had a blast.

***

I considered myself to be an evangelical pastor, though no longer a fundamentalist. Definitions of evangelical vary depending on who you ask. Sometimes it refers to people who insist on a fairly literal interpretation of the Bible. These are generalities, but evangelicals usually profess belief in a literal heaven and a literal hell. They often subscribe to the belief that the Bible is without error and that inasmuch as it addresses issues of science and history, it is accurate. Therefore, the theory of evolution is generally rejected in favor of creationism. I did not outwardly repudiate these beliefs, but neither did I emphasize them.

I preached about a personal relationship with God, and I sought this myself. I read the Bible and other devotional books to help me feel closer to God. I led church members in the course "Knowing God." I attended the weekly meeting of the more moderate Baptist pastors in the area. I craved a faith relevant to a person's life, to my life. This critical eye as to who was or was not a strict adherent to a particular approach to the Bible and faith was something that I had experienced and examined thoroughly and rejected. I had seen its underbelly. I enjoyed the moderate pastors' group, even serving as president one year.

I tried to bring as much music as possible into the church. Most of the Chinese children took music lessons; many studied the violin or piano. On special occasions, such as Easter or Thanksgiving, I put together an orchestra to perform and play along with the congregation. The young people whose skills were adequate played the piano during the services. I also started a choir for the Mandarin-speaking members. Someone donated some money to the church music ministry, and I used it to purchase a set of choir chimes and formed a handbell choir that performed periodically.

Occasionally other Chinese churches invited me to speak. I developed a seminar on the subject of Chinese immigrant parents understanding their American children. This was enthusiastically received. I mixed in a lot of humor with my talks which I delivered in Mandarin.

At a board meeting one evening, the most senior elder presented a list of duties for the pastor along with a directive that I present a plan of initiatives for each year to be approved by the elders. I surveyed the room. An elder with whom I was close personally kept his head bowed, avoiding eye contact with me. This was perplexing and frankly insulting.

I had been their pastor for five years, and the church had grown substantially. We had even purchased adjoining property and constructed an additional parking lot to accommodate the increased attendance.

While I performed all the duties specified in the document, it didn't seem to take into account the myriad of other things I did as I shepherded this flock of believers. Told to present my sermon topics six months in advance for approval, it appeared this was the elders' way of establishing their authority. I found it difficult to be someone's leader while, at the same time, taking orders from them.

***

We visited BR at the University of North Carolina, where he majored in music. He showed us around the large campus and took us to the campus bookstore, and while Kathy, Margaret and Daniel shopped for hats and shirts displaying Tarheels, I found my way to the textbook section, walking down aisle after aisle of books, wondering what it would have been like to study great thinkers of various disciplines.

My eyes landed on a book, *Genesis: A Living Conversation*, by Bill Moyers. Moyers discussed the stories of Genesis with thinkers from many disciplines: theologians, historians, poets, psychologists, philosophers and others. They were from Christian, Jewish and Muslim backgrounds and they discussed the stories of Genesis; Adam and Eve, Noah, Abraham and others. I purchased the book.

When I returned home, I could hardly put the book down. For the first time, I heard varied interpretations of these biblical accounts. While each saw the value of such stories, none insisted the events were historically accurate or held some absolute theological meaning.

So this was what it would be like to study and preach from the bible without being tethered to fundamentalist interpretation and dogma. Could I take this approach in my preaching? I decided to try.

32

In 1999, I went to Israel with a tour company that offered an eight-day trip for clergy at a low price. I made my way across the ancient stones toward the wall that separates the Jewish section from the Muslim section where the Dome of the Rock stands. Ahead, scores of people crowded against the Wailing Wall, portions of which some believe go back to the time of Solomon. There were many men dressed in black; they wore long beards with curls falling down from under their black hats. The custom was to write your prayers on tiny slips of paper and stick them into the cracks in the wall. Men of all ages, including young boys, did this and stood rocking back and forth, praying.

As I approached the wall wearing the paper yarmulke I'd been given, I unexpectedly began to cry. The energy, pain, sorrow and hope in this place were palpable. I wedged my prayer between two of the rugged stones. My emotions swept me away again when another pastor baptized me in the Jordan River. We visited Bethlehem, the Dead Sea, Masada, the Church of the Holy Sepulcher, Gethsemane, etc. I swam in the Dead Sea. While my feelings about the dogma of Christianity hadn't changed, I was awed by being in a place where so many people had come for centuries, seeking spiritual guidance.

We visited a church called The Church of the White Fathers, which was known for its unusual acoustics. The tour guide asked for a volunteer to sing so that we could experience the striking acoustics of the building. When no one else stepped forward, I volunteered. After that, I was the go-to singer of the group. When we visited an ancient outdoor Roman amphitheater at Caesarea on the Mediterranean Sea, they asked me to stand at the bottom and sing, allowing tourists to experience the natural amplification effect.

I returned to my work at the church with renewed enthusiasm. We held a series of strategic planning meetings. Many of the older members wished we could build a nicer building. The church had celebrated one hundred years of history, but it had never had a proper building. The one we used was a repurposed army barracks.

I advocated for a nicer building among the church leaders. At a meeting, one particular member who had been away in another city for much of my tenure was adamant that money should be spent on mission work and not on a building. Before his diatribe, most of the leaders were willing to discuss a new building, but they acquiesced to his opposition.

I felt the man's attitude was disrespectful to the faithful members who had supported the church for decades.

"If you feel it is inappropriate to spend money on a building instead of sending it to missions, why don't you sell the lovely home that you and your wife live in, give the money to missions and live in your car?" I said to him in front of the other leaders.

As a reaction to my words, he wrote a letter to the elders requesting that I be disciplined or censored for behavior unbecoming of a pastor. The elders agreed with him that it was inappropriate for me to say what I did. They wrote me a letter of reprimand. I acted as if it didn't faze me.

But the conflict took its toll on me mentally and emotionally. It became a struggle to function. Kathy grew concerned. One night, without my knowledge, she phoned a young former church member who was a physician whom she knew admired me and told him some of what was going on and that I was not doing well. He came to our house, sat with me and we talked for a while. I appreciated his support.

I decided to ask my family doctor for the antidepressant medication that I had previously taken. I had stopped therapy and medication after Taiwan, but now I needed it again. *Am I going backward?*

"What did those people do to you?" Maryann, my therapist, asked me. She tried to understand why I appeared to be falling apart. I had started seeing her for therapy a couple of years after we moved to Virginia Beach. She was a wonderful person and a tremendous help to me. What I described was hard for her to grasp.

I had difficulty facing each day. Often on my way to the church on weekdays, I drove to a park, sat in my car and went through mindfulness breathing exercises in an effort to steel myself for the day. I didn't think I could go on, so I asked my doctor to write a letter for a medical leave. Dr. Espada did so without hesitation.

I sat alone in the old motor-court motel room on the oceanfront in Virginia Beach. It was unusual for it to snow, even in January, but it did that year. A pastor friend said one of his church members liked to help clergy and had agreed to pay for the room. I stayed there for a week. Kathy came and visited me several times. She was scared and wasn't sure what was happening. She handled everything at home without me. Daniel spent the night with me one night, and we watched a basketball game together.

I was at a low point. The snow falling on the beach looked surreal. I was confused and lonely. I never stopped praying and reading the Bible and Christian literature. Some might conclude my movement away from orthodox faith resulted from some back-sliding or lack of devotion. This was never the case.

After using up my stay at the motel, I packed another suitcase and headed out to a farm in central Virginia that allowed pastors to come and stay free of charge. I wrote in my journal, read and roamed the grounds of the farm.

I realized my depression and my faith outlook might be connected. Was my faith dilemma causing my depression, or was my mood problem fueling the gloomy outlook on my vocation as a pastor?

In psychology, human behavior and thought are studied, and theories are then constructed to explain the human experience. The graduate work I pursued in counseling followed this model. Theology, on the other hand, takes an externally received dogma (scripture and tradition) and uses it to explain people, their problems and behaviors.

It wasn't the studies in psychology that drew me away from orthodox faith. Rather, it was the inadequacy of religion that drove me to psychology for answers.

As the end of my sabbatical grew closer, I felt somewhat stronger and vowed to give priority to my mental health, physical health, and general state of mind and not allow the many opinions thrown at me by church leaders to ever bring me again to such a dark place.

"Did you get what you were looking for here?" the farmer asked as I put my suitcase in my car.

"I hope so," I said.

I returned to my duties. Church leaders handled me with kid gloves for a while. I was determined to find a way out of this situation—out of the ministry.

Margaret had started college in another city in Virginia. Two children in college now, and one in high school. I had no other profession to pursue. To just quit would be irresponsible. Kathy had a good job, but her salary alone couldn't sustain us.

I had my master's degree in counseling, but I wasn't yet licensed. I had slowly accumulated counseling hours toward the number required in order to sit for the exam, but I wasn't anywhere close. We owned a home, had three cars and tried to give our children the best life possible. The fact was that the church paid me pretty well. I had to try to hang on until I could finish my doctoral studies.

33

"Will you consider becoming our pastor?" A deacon from a small Chinese mission church in northern Virginia approached me. The small church near Washington, DC, had started a few years earlier and was considered a mission church because financial support came from another church and the state Baptist association. I had been there a couple of times as a guest speaker.

I proposed that I make the three-hour drive to the Washington, DC, area each week on Thursday and stay through Sunday. This allowed me time to meet the one-year residency requirement at William & Mary and complete my dissertation.

In July of 2000, I submitted my resignation to the church in Virginia Beach and accepted the offer from the mission church.

"Papa, I'm so proud of you. Go spread your knowledge all over northern Virginia." These words Daniel, now seventeen, wrote on a card he gave me when I began traveling each week. For the next two years, I attended church activities in the evenings, Thursday through Saturday, and visited members and prospects during the day. Sundays were full with services in the morning and often some event in the afternoon before I drove home Sunday night.

Kathy occasionally went with me but couldn't leave her job or Daniel on a regular basis. By now, both BR and Margaret were away at college. Kathy found the house to be so empty, she took in a boarder for a period of time.

For the first year, I stayed with a gracious and kind church member during my days away from home. But since I was serving as the pastor of their church, I didn't feel relaxed. I usually got up and left to go to the church in the morning and didn't come home until bedtime. Later, I rented a room in someone's home.

Sometimes it felt like whiplash, spending the first part of the week in a very secular university setting and then transitioning to the extremely religious context of a group of Chinese people who were new to Christianity.

One evening I had just arrived in northern Virginia and was about to get in bed. My cell phone rang. It was a young man who had recently joined the church along with his wife. I didn't know them well.

"My wife has just had a baby," he said, seeming a bit nervous. "Do you think you could come over to the hospital and pray for our daughter? She is three months premature."

"I can be there in about forty minutes." I pulled into the parking garage of the huge Fairfax General Hospital and began searching for the Neonatal Intensive Care Unit. When I arrived, I recognized the Chinese couple standing over an incubator. The couple motioned for me to come into the glass-enclosed area. A nurse reached into the incubator through holes in the plexiglass and attached some kind of tube to the tiny infant, who was barely bigger than the nurse's hand, maybe eight to ten inches long.

"Mu shi, xie xie ni lai." (Pastor, thank you for coming.)

"How is she?" I asked. Guessing the situation was critical, I was cautious as to what I said.

"We are hopeful," the young man said. "She is stable. Will you pray for her?" His wife looked at me expectantly.

The couple asked the nurse to take the baby out of the incubator and indicated they wanted me to hold the child. Maybe because it was my custom to hold newborns during baby dedication, the first-time parents brought a child to church. They anticipated me doing so now.

I had no special power to enable this fragile creature to live, but I didn't want to disappoint them. I carefully cradled the little girl in the palms of my hands, careful not to disturb the various tubes connecting her to life-sustaining equipment. Her tiny diaper was probably no more than three inches square.

"Our loving heavenly father, touch this little child and if it is your will, let her live." I prayed earnestly. As I drove home, I had difficulty believing the infant could survive. These young parents viewed me as a link to God who could sustain their child's life. *Am I a link to God?*

I visited the child numerous times during the next three months as she gradually developed. The proud parents brought their daughter to church the first Sunday after discharge from the hospital. I stood at the front of the church and held her in my arms, praying that God would bless this child and her young parents. They were convinced that my prayer that day in the hospital had saved the child's life.

As I had experienced at previous churches, the consistent presence of a pastor resulted in church membership growing. We began to fill the fellowship hall. The American church that sponsored the Chinese mission gave me an office alongside their other pastors.

We periodically had a joint service (Chinese and American). This was cumbersome since everything had to be translated. Our host church, while Baptist, had a more liturgical-style service than was customary in the Baptist churches in which I had grown up and with which I had been associated for the most part. Prayers were recited in unison, and communion involved walking to the front of the church rather than having a plate passed around. While growing up as a Baptist, it was not uncommon to hear amen occasionally from the congregation, and preachers could be known to shout. But this church was quite sedate.

The Chinese people in my congregation, largely new to Christianity and mostly from mainland China, were used to a method of worship in which the teachings of the faith were stated in a straightforward manner. Western Christians have heard about Christ's birth, death and resurrection for so long that many sermons on these subjects emphasize abstract meanings. For our Chinese members, they wanted to hear that these were historical events.

The stories of Moses, Abraham, Jacob, Gideon, Joshua and others offer accounts of the journey of a people of faith. Indeed, some say these were myths created to give people a sense of identity and to carry on the lessons of their faith.

I began to take this approach to preaching and felt a certain freedom. I emphasized the lessons we could learn in our modern times. I did not say that I did not accept the Bible as literally true. I just did not emphasize the teachings that such a view necessitated.

The challenge came from members of my congregation whose families had observed the Christian faith for generations and did not accept this metaphorical approach. When they embraced Christianity, they rejected the cultural perspectives of their families and countries of origin. In some cases, they had been rejected by their family for their decision. By and large, the Chinese preachers they heard at conferences and other churches emphasized that the Bible is to be understood in a straightforward, literal manner, not symbolically or metaphorically.

I held a prayer meeting when the United States prepared to invade Afghanistan in 2001. A small group of seven or eight members gathered, and we talked about what we would pray for: our military, their families, our leaders. I mentioned that we should pray for the people of Afghanistan.

"Why should we pray for them? They are the enemies of God!" one participant said. While this view seems extreme, herein lies the difficulty in being a Biblical literalist. I explained that commands to annihilate one's enemies, etc., were given to Israel for a particular time and situation and weren't necessarily applicable for us today. But such words appear in the Bible, as are many other things that are frankly disturbing.

The Baptist church that housed the Chinese church was a moderate church. That is, it did not emphasize a rigidly literal interpretation of the Bible. There was openness to women in ministry. This church was affiliated with the Cooperative Baptist Fellowship rather than the more fundamentalist Southern Baptist Convention. I felt comfortable here.

The church that hosted my Chinese congregation offered BR an internship as a youth worker for six months after he graduated from the University of North Carolina in the spring 2001. He had been heavily involved in the Baptist student ministry in college, so he was at home in this role.

***

Kathy and I were surprised when BR decided to join the army in a delayed entry program. He didn't see much of a path forward in singing, and the army promised to help him pay off his student debt.

Since he could speak Mandarin, the Army told him that he could be a linguist. When he took the language learning aptitude test, he did so well that the Army decided to train him to be an Arabic linguist.

During those six months before entering the army, BR and I rented an apartment together near the church. We ate sardines and ramen noodles many evenings. During my years in conservative Christianity, I had never partaken in drinking alcohol of any kind. Now, BR and I sometimes got a six-pack of Rolling Rock beer and enjoyed a few in our bachelor pad.

I was back home one Monday and noticed that Cinnamon had gotten very thin. "Has Cinnamon been eating?" I asked Kathy.

"Yes, he eats all of his food," she said.

I tried to get him to do his roll-over trick, offering him a treat. He tried but couldn't. The next day I took him to the vet. When the vet called, his voice sounded serious.

"I have your dog on the operating table, and it doesn't look good. It's cancer, and it's everywhere." He could tell I was at a loss for what to say, and after a long pause, he said, "Mr. McDonald, I don't think Cinnamon is going to be with us much longer."

We buried Cinnamon in our backyard. Margaret and Daniel put a few of his toys and his sweater in his cardboard coffin. We sobbed as we held hands and said goodbye. He had been with us for eleven years.

***

I had started my drive home to Virginia Beach one Sunday afternoon when my cell phone rang. "Hi Marg, what's up?"

"We are at the hospital. Something is wrong with Mama," she said. "We were out shopping, and she started acting funny."

"What do you mean, funny?" I asked.

"At first, I thought she was mad at me or something. She just stared at me and wouldn't answer me. I thought maybe she got too hot."

"Put her on the phone and let me talk to her," I said.

"Well . . . she is not responding right now," Margaret said.

"What?" I said.

"We are waiting for the results of some tests. Just get here as soon as you can." She sounded frightened.

I felt terrified and helpless. As I traveled home, I prayed for Kathy and regretted every moment I had ever been impatient or irritable with her. I was angry that I was away from her.

This was the first of a series of seizures. Kathy began a series of visits to neurologists, had several MRI's, and various medication trials. Eventually, the right treatment was found. The problem had first occurred when Kathy and Margaret were in an antique shop. Kathy apparently bought a chest but has no recollection of making the purchase. The chest now sits in our foyer, and we affectionately refer to it as the *seizure chest*.

34

In August of 2002, we sold our house in Virginia Beach and moved to the Washington, DC, area. I had been commuting weekly for two years. We purchased a new townhouse which was under construction. We lived in the home of a family who had been out of the country for six months.

By now, BR was in the army, Margaret had returned to college, now at Virginia Commonwealth University in Richmond, and Daniel started at Virginia Tech. Kathy secured a position as a coordinator in the public school system. It was an administrative position, and she was ideally suited for it. I began my duties as a full-time pastor, while continuing classes at William & Mary, now one hundred miles south.

"Daddy is in the hospital, maybe a stroke," Mom said as we spoke by phone. I flew to Mobile. Daddy was largely unresponsive and couldn't eat.

"Son, help me to the men's room," he repeatedly said. He had a catheter, and this was not necessary. "I want to lay in the front bedroom," he said several times.

Seeing Daddy in this state turned my thoughts to what I knew about his nervous breakdown as a young man. I could only imagine how he suffered then. My subsequent studies have led me to the conclusion that Daddy likely suffered from Obsessive-Compulsive Disorder. People with OCD experience intrusive, often abhorrent thoughts. This should not be confused with Obsessive-Compulsive Personality Disorder, which refers to an individual who is extremely rigid and orderly, though some individuals suffer from both.

Today, medication can be extremely helpful, sometimes almost miraculous, in treating individuals suffering from OCD. Psychotherapy can be an effective treatment as well. Unfortunately, neither was available to Daddy in the 1940s. The electro-convulsive therapy apparently helped Daddy, but it changed his personality and resulted in him often stuttering when he spoke, a condition that continued throughout his life.

Mom and I were on our way home from the hospital, having just met with the doctor, who said that if it were his father, he wouldn't take any more measures to try to save him. Mom began to cry. She talked about how she and Daddy used to kneel down by their bed and say their prayers together when they were first married. She talked about the walks they took. I had never heard her talk like this.

"We were so happy," she sobbed. They had been married for sixty years.

Daddy lingered, and after a couple of weeks, I returned to my duties at the church in Virginia. My father's imminent death affected me deeply. I called BR and cried.

"How can we just let him die?" I asked BR.

"I know, Papa," he said. "I'm so sorry."

"If you want to see Daddy, you probably should come now," my brother Joe said when he phoned two weeks after I returned to Virginia. I slept in his hospital room the first night back in Mobile. He may have acknowledged that I was there. I can't be sure.

He stopped breathing for long periods of time, sometimes up to twenty seconds, then took a deep breath with great difficulty. I watched this for several hours. When the nurse came to turn him, I noticed how small and lifeless he was. The periods between breaths became longer and longer. Finally, he didn't breathe. I called the nurse, who listened for a heartbeat and told me that he had passed. He was eighty-seven years old.

Joe and I went with Mom to the funeral home to make arrangements for the funeral. Now eighty-six years old, Mom listened silently as Joe and I discussed the details.

She slowly opened her purse and pulled out a checkbook. "We had prepared to pay for this," she said. "How much will it be?" her hands shaking slightly, her voice frail but steady. She and Daddy had always watched their money carefully, always self-sufficient.

For some reason, her stoicism impacted me deeply. Mom and Daddy had never had a particularly loving or affectionate relationship, at least not during the time that I can remember. But they had promised to be faithful until death—and they were.

When Daddy had his nervous breakdown early in their marriage, a doctor told my mother he was insane and may be dangerous and that she shouldn't stay with him. Daddy's family told her that she shouldn't expect any help from them.

But Mom stayed and saw Daddy through his illness, and together the two of them provided a good life for Joe and me. My mother could be difficult and somewhat controlling, and it often bothered me that she was bossy with Daddy. But I'll never fully know what they went through. Perhaps she took on that demeanor when Daddy couldn't function. Mom did what had to be done then, and sitting with pen and checkbook, she did what had to be done now.

After the funeral, I returned to the church and assumed my duties as pastor. For a while, I dreamed that Daddy had not really died, that everything was fine. Hearing that someone has lost a parent is an almost daily occurrence, but now my own parent's death felt unbearable. For a few years after that, I said that I hadn't dealt adequately with my father's death. Now I understand that it is not possible to really accept the loss of one's parent. It just hurts less as time goes on.

For our twenty-fifth wedding anniversary, Kathy bought me a new trombone. I had played the old one since high school. I joined the symphony affiliated with the local community college for one year and found a brass ensemble led by a former military musician. Kathy began to make new friends through her job. We started over once again.

One Monday, I picked Kathy up at the airport when she returned from a trip to Mobile. When she got in the car, she had a little carrier containing a tiny puppy, no bigger than my hand. Jazzie, a toy poodle, became a source of joy, often snuggling with us in bed as we adjusted to our empty nest.

***

By early 2003, I had finished all the classes for my Ph.D. and working on my dissertation research. I drove back to Williamsburg once a month to meet with a cohort of students and confer with the chair of my dissertation committee.

Throughout my doctoral program, we had examined various developmental theories—how an individual develops in various domains, e.g., cognitive, moral, emotional, social. Some years before, I came across Faith Development Theory, which had opened the door for me to understand the changes in my religious beliefs.

According to this theory, encounters with others impact faith outlook, and in turn, one's faith outlook influences one's relationship with other people. I can certainly identify people who helped form my faith outlook in various ways. Granny praised me for going to church and being a good boy. I never wanted to disappoint her. My relationship with Mr. Coleman triggered my questioning of racist attitudes during my formative years.

While my relationship with my religion deteriorated, I held on to it for so long partly because of my relationship with the people who maintained expectations of me. Even my relationship with Kathy was a factor. As I embraced a faith approach, she stood by me as my faith changed. Had she cautioned me about turning from the faith, the ultimate decision to leave the church would have been much harder.

Through my years in ministry, I encountered others with completely different life outlooks and beliefs. I loved the people of Taiwan, and my relationship with its culture caused me to question further whether what I believed was the only way. What was happening to me was actually normal, healthy and to be expected.

I submitted a dissertation proposal to study faith development among members of the clergy. This was a rather novel area of study for a person pursuing a doctoral degree in counseling at a secular university. My committee approved the topic.

I conducted in-depth interviews with pastors. Kathy spent hours transcribing them. I analyzed the transcripts and placed each pastor in a stage according to Faith Development Theory. I identified those clergy who had advanced to higher levels of faith outlook.

I wanted to know how such clergy functioned in the role of leader while evolving in their own beliefs. Does movement away from certainty make one a better pastor, or should it result in looking for a different career.

One finding was that these later-stage pastors had become comfortable with uncertainty. For most, this happened during seminary education. They were permitted to question or reject certain viewpoints. This had not been my experience.

In addition, each of the pastors had a companion during their journey. Someone walked with them as they searched and questioned. I had this to a degree with Bill, Dr. Decker, Maryann and other therapists. But for me, I struggled to bridge the chasm between my ministry and these discussions with my mentors.

As I poured over my research, I examined my own role. I had invested so much time and training in this calling. *Is there a way to be at peace with my journey and continue to shepherd a flock?*

***

For years, I secretly kept a picture of myself in my top dresser drawer, one of those grainy black and white photos that you got by sitting in one of those booths in a shopping center, closing the curtain, and putting a few coins in the machine. Under my face, I had written the words Brian R. McDonald, Ph.D. In May 2004, my dream became a reality.

Mom came for the ceremony at the College of William & Mary. I wish Daddy could have been there. Daddy always lacked the ability to express emotion normally. When encountering something emotionally charged, his face contorted as if in some kind of pain. This had happened when I took him to see his parents' grave not long before he died.

"It was a mistake to have come here," he said, his face twisted in anguish. Sometimes it was because of something touching, like the time I showed him the video of BR singing "Oh What a Beautiful Morning" in his high school musical *Oklahoma*.

If Daddy had been there to see me receive my degree, I imagined his face would have displayed that anguished look that I would know meant he was moved emotionally. Mom, now eighty-eight years old, was proud, but she had been bragging to her friends for years that I had a Ph.D. when I really didn't. Now that it was true, it may have felt somewhat anti-climactic to her. Sometimes I heard her say that she studied at the University of Southern Mississippi. Actually, she attended some summer workshops there a few times. But she made the most of those experiences.

"You have to hold your head up," I remember her often telling me.

Mom died a few years later at the age of ninety-three.

Smart, talented, creative and ambitious, I'll always wonder what her life could have been if she had lived at a different time.

I've never heard anyone play the piano like she did.

35

The last few months had been a marathon as I completed and defended my dissertation in order to graduate. I had achieved the goal of earning my Ph.D., a quest that had dictated much of our lives since returning from Taiwan twelve years prior. As far as my role at the church, I had been on autopilot.

I sat in my office at the church, my bible open on my desk. I needed to prepare my sermon for Sunday, but I couldn't wrap my head around the task. Something had shifted inside me. *I just can't keep doing this.* Now, I struggled to summon the will to even go through the motions.

There had been a conflict brewing in the church during the past couple of months. Churches have politics, factions and conflict; it is inevitable. So often, I heard pastors say that it was their belief in their calling that got them through these trying times. I had long ago abandoned the belief in my calling to the ministry. I needed to smooth some ruffled feathers, and the problem should blow over. It was part of the job—but I didn't want to.

"What if I just resign now?" I said to Kathy. "There are still a few steps that I have to take to be licensed as a counselor in Virginia. It would be easier to do those things if I didn't have to be a pastor."

I taught a graduate class one evening per week the previous semester for Johns Hopkins University at their Rockville, Maryland, campus. I was pretty sure I could keep doing that.

"We can get by financially for a few months with me teaching and you continuing your job." I assured her. Kathy knew the discontent I had experienced in the ministry for so long.

After thirty years in ministry, I willingly walked away. Not unlike the prodigal son, I was returning home—hopefully to the uncomplicated faith that had started me on this journey.

***

Kathy and I open the door, and Jazzie enthusiastically greets us, oblivious to the emotionally draining event we had just experienced, leaving the church for the last time. Thrilled we have returned, she jumps into Kathy's arms, and we sit down together in the living room, accepting her unconditional love and comfort.

The days and weeks that followed were filled with uncertainty. I had negotiated three months' salary when I resigned, but it was going to be uncertain after that. But it was a new beginning and a time to begin re-making myself.

While getting started as a counselor, I had various part-time jobs, some related to research analysis, which I had studied during my graduate work. I did Chinese translation work for the courts and government. I tried my hand at formulating test questions for standardized tests. I worked at Starbucks as a barista for a while, hanging out with a bunch of twenty-somethings. I even got a tattoo.

It took a year before I started being paid as a counselor and another year after that before it provided a steady income. It was an indescribable relief to be free from the expectation to be someone that I no longer felt I could or wanted to be.

I increased my involvement playing trombone, joining a jazz band, something I had dreamed of doing for years. On one occasion, the band played at the Kennedy Center in Washington, DC, for a New Year's Eve celebration. What a thrill.

I continued to teach classes as an adjunct professor at Johns Hopkins University and also at George Mason University. I relished the environment of a university, me as a professor. I had a new identity.

***

A tale has been told for generations about a rabbi who one day decided to take a walk in the woods near the synagogue. After walking for quite some time, he realized that he had lost his way and did not know the way back. He tried and tried to find his way out of the forest but to no avail. As he was searching for the way out, he happened upon a group of people whom he recognized as members of his congregation.

"We are so happy to see you, Rabbi. We are lost and cannot find our way out of the forest. Can you show us the way out?" The rabbi thought for a moment, stroking his beard.

"I'm afraid I cannot show you the path out of the forest, but I can show you many paths that do not lead out," he said. Not unlike this rabbi, I searched for years for a way out of the morass I found myself in. I tried and tried to reconcile Christian doctrine with what my conscience told me. I now know many paths that lead nowhere, at least for me.

In another telling of the above fable, the rabbi says, "I don't know the way, but I will walk with you as we search for it together." Maybe if it had been acceptable for me to admit that I had the misgivings I did, I could have continued to be a pastor. Perhaps that could happen in a liberal denomination that allowed for that kind of latitude. There is no way that could have happened in the conservative evangelical environment in which I served.

A few years after my resignation, I was looking for something in a closet and came across my framed ordination certificate. In addition to my name, date and some formal words about ordination, it had the signatures of the pastors who examined me and the deacons and pastor who laid hands on me to ordain me. My thoughts returned to that day and the admonition against ever turning from the beliefs I had affirmed.

The lettering for my name had faded over the nearly thirty years since it was penned. The calligrapher had made my name look like some important personage by embellishing each letter with little curls and flairs. Apparently, a different pen was used for the embellishments because they had faded more than the letters themselves so that they were now barely visible. Now it was just me, nothing extra.

I can't return to being the person I was before this journey began. I wouldn't want to. I probed the depths of faith and belief. All of it, along with what I have done and experienced, has made me who I am. But the longing to be true to myself steadily gained momentum over the years until I finally surrendered.

Afterword

As I searched my memories to write this memoir, I realized that for much of my life I had kept many of my inner thoughts and reservations to myself. I believed that to reveal them would bring shame and possible rejection by those who employed me or looked up to me.

I now see that this started in high school when I couldn't accept the teaching about hell and found that questioning this only brought admonitions from more mature believers. My rejection of this horrifying fate of non-believers became a secret that I never disclosed.

For years, I longed for a time when I could be authentic, not needing to weigh my words lest I surprise or disappoint someone who looked to me as their faith leader. I suppose I got used to being duplicitous. But it was not out of any desire to deceive. My hope was that it would all eventually make sense, allowing me to be open and transparent.

Now I am free to be myself and express my hard-won beliefs. It is incredibly freeing. But now, I feel the need to hide something else. As I encounter people in my work as a therapist or university professor, I don't want them to know that I attended the schools I did or professed the dogma that I once professed. What will others think of me if they learn that I once subscribed to a belief system that is in so many ways judgmental and intolerant of people?

Kathy and I now attend a church (though not every Sunday) that is about as different from our years of experience as one could imagine. I consider myself a follower of the teachings of Jesus, whose teachings did impact my life greatly. Jesus's teaching of the value of each human has defined my life outlook. I prefer not to call myself a Christian. That term embodies too much that I have left behind.

Our Family Today

BR, our oldest, was in the army for eight years and was awarded the Bronze Star for his efforts in the war on terror. He founded a non-profit that assists veterans who hope to find a career in the arts. He now works in New York City for a company that makes communication equipment used by the military and law enforcement. Being the oldest, he may have absorbed more of the pervasive religious environment of the early years of our home. He is on his own journey to sort it out and is working on his own memoir. He and Leigh, his significant other, live in Tewksbury Township, New Jersey.

Margaret finished college with a degree in Art Education. She is in her sixteenth year as a teacher in the same school district where Kathy works. She is amazing at what she does, having developed methods to teach art to children who have learning and developmental disorders. She may be the kindest human being I've ever known. She and her wife Nicole live not far away in a Washington, DC, suburb.

Daniel is an officer with the US Navy Civil Engineering Corps. He and his wife Rosie have three children (twelve, ten and five) and are currently stationed in Virginia Beach, where coincidently, all three of our children graduated from high school. From the time he was a child, Daniel took things apart to see how they worked. Being an engineer for the navy is a perfect place for him. He plays trumpet, and we get together to jam whenever we can.

Kathy is now a teacher of English as a second language in the public schools. After being a school administrator for many years, she has enjoyed stepping back to something not so demanding. She feels so at home with the children and their families from various cultures.

One of our children, when reading a manuscript of this book, said, "Papa may be the main character of this book, but Mama is the *hero*." I concur.

"I'm so sorry for all that I put you through as I tried to figure out my faith." I said to Kathy as she finished reading the manuscript.

"It's been an adventure. I don't regret anything we have done," she assured me.

I enjoy immensely watching Kathy be Grandmama to our grandchildren. I am now Grandpops, my favorite of all the titles I have ever had. Kathy and I enjoy sailing on the weekends when we can get away. I have a private psychotherapy practice and see around twenty-five clients each week. I love my office in historic Old Town Alexandria, Virginia.

In 2018, our family (ten of us) met in Taiwan and visited the home where we once lived, the Lei Hu church where I was once pastor, and the schools the children attended. We found people who still remembered us after twenty-six years. Our house looked mostly the same. If I closed my eyes, I could imagine *Shao Hei* wagging her tail and waiting just inside the gate.

We attended a service at the Lei Hu Church. We were able to visit with Arnie, our dear former colleague who is still in Taiwan. Debbie has passed away. Our old housekeeper Chou Tai Tai, who tracked us down a couple of years ago and called us, said that for more than twenty years, she asked every missionary she met if they knew missionaries named McDonald. Finally, a teacher at Morrison Academy saw Kathy's name on a Facebook post and told Chou Tai Tai that she might have found the family she was looking for. We visited Chou Tai Tai and her husband in their home. It was like finding a long-lost relative.

We took a picture of our family, now doubled in size since we lived in Taiwan, standing in front of the red gate of our former home. It felt surreal.

When asked where their hometown is, BR, Margaret and Daniel say Taichung, Taiwan.

McDonald Family in front of Lei Hu Church, 1987.

McDonald Family in front of Lei Hu church, 2018.

Acknowledgments

For several years I recorded my thoughts about my life in the ministry. I wrote for my own understanding, rarely considering a larger audience. First, I must thank my son BR who first urged me to write a memoir. I devoted most Saturdays to this effort, pecking away at my laptop for hours at a coffee shop.

In 2019, BR organized a phone conference with Jill Swenson of Swenson Book Development, to discuss the possibility of publishing my story. She agreed to read my manuscript. When reading her meticulously written assessment, one phrase leaped out at me, "I'm clearly a fan." I was thrilled that someone who reads scores of books considered my story worth telling.

There was hard work ahead. Scores of emails, dozens of calls, Skype sessions, always more revisions, and voracious reading of other memoirists. This went on for almost two years. "Show, don't tell!" Jill said repeatedly. I am grateful for her firm, but patient hand.

I want to thank Ian Graham Leask of Calumet Editions for believing that there was an audience for this book. Many thanks to Calumet's staff, Gary Lindberg for the beautiful jacket design and layout, and Beth Williams for her careful editing.

I am indebted to my own therapists over the years, without whose guidance I would never have gained the perspective I now have. My own therapy clients have reinforced my belief in the value of probing our life stories.

My wife Kathy has been my strength throughout the nearly 50 years we have been together, and this project was no exception. Thank you Kathy for your patience during the many hours I spent on this project and for your keen memory of events when mine failed.

"How's the book going Papa?" was a common greeting from my three children. They are the greatest.

About the Author

Brian Rush McDonald grew up in Alabama, gave up his dream of becoming a musician to become a Jesus freak, and graduated from Bob Jones University. He spent nearly thirty years as a preacher, missionary, and pastor, including seven years in Taiwan where he learned to speak Mandarin Chinese. He earned a master's degree from Liberty University and completed his Ph.D. at the College of William & Mary. He has taught at Johns Hopkins University and George Mason University as an adjunct professor of counseling. He plays trombone in several local bands, both classical and jazz. He and his wife Kathy have been married for 44 years. They enjoy sailing together on the Chesapeake Bay. They have three adult children and three grandchildren. McDonald is a psychotherapist in private practice in Alexandria, Virginia.

Made in United States
Orlando, FL
25 August 2022

21556098R00157